**JB JOSSEY-BASS™**
A Wiley Brand

# 76 Ways to Increase Special Event Attendance

Scott C. Stevenson, Editor

**WILEY**

978-1-118-69217-2        ISBN

978-1-118-70389-2        ISBN (online)

# 76 Ways to Increase Special Event Attendance

Published by

**Stevenson, Inc.**

P.O. Box 4528 • Sioux City, Iowa • 51104
Phone 712.239.3010 • Fax 712.239.2166

www.stevensoninc.com

# 76 Ways to Increase Special Event Attendance

## Table of Contents

## Table of Contents

# 76 Ways to Increase Special Event Attendance

## 1. Pull Out All the Stops in Planning Your Event

The best way to guarantee great attendance is to give people an awesome event. Start from square one to accomplish just that:

✓ Appoint an enthusiastic chairperson.

✓ Make your planning committee a mix of both creative people who can come up with ideas and "work horses" great at follow-through.

✓ Don't rely solely on your traditional volunteer base; ask the regulars to bring a friend to brainstorming sessions or committee meetings. Or add to that important core group by calling in donors, clients, alumni and others to fuel the creative flame. Involving new people brings forth fresh ideas and creates a longer list of names to pull out come ticket-selling time.

### Promotion Idea

Create an event to promote an event. For example, hold a pre-event hour that gives the public a taste of what's to come and invite members of the press to be on hand.

**ADMIT ONE**

## 2. Maximize Pre-event Coverage To Boost Event Attendance

Your local newspaper may be agreeable to covering your special event on the day it occurs, but advance publicity that can help boost attendance may be harder to get.

The following are several strategies for enlisting your local newspaper's help ahead of time.

❏ **Choose before or after.** Since news space and staff time are limited, ask for either advance publicity or event coverage rather than insisting on both. Follow up with one or two great photos of your event and a brief release outlining attendance, funds raised and how they will be used.

❏ **Set a realistic but unprecedented goal.** Contact the paper to tell them you hope to boost last year's fundraising total by a record-setting amount, explaining increased community needs for your programs and services with a local angle.

❏ **Let others tell your story.** Ask one or two people who have benefitted from your organization to give interviews about how funds raised from last year's event helped pay for their job training, holiday dinner or back-to-school supplies for their children. Newspapers like inspiring, human-interest stories. Make the connection to your event clear by arranging the interviews and providing background.

❏ **Invite them to be a sponsor.** Like any business, newspapers seek ways to contribute to their communities. Ask them to become an event sponsor with full benefits, but with a combination of advertising and money. When they promote your event, they will be promoting themselves.

❏ **Create an advertising supplement.** Most newspapers have frequent inserts. A sponsor-funded flyer or brochure can be a highly cost-effective way to reach a broad audience.

❏ **Cultivate your contacts.** Develop a friendly bond with the staff most likely to cover your organization's events. Send positive notes or e-mails complimenting them on other articles and let them know you take an interest in their section and work in general. Stay in touch even when you don't want something.

## 3. Set the Bar High by Offering Something New

To give your annual event a welcome change from past years, assign your planning committee to come up with one great way to add flair to this year's event. Be sure and talk about it in invitations and pre-event publicity. Ideas:

- Offer a great donated prize or access to a popular guest or celebrity;

- Move to a location that is an experience in itself — a lavish outdoor garden or arboretum, a festively decorated hotel banquet room or theatre;

- Present food with a flourish — advertise beforehand that guests will enjoy display cooking with area chefs, an elaborate dessert buffet prepared by local bakers and candy makers, or that local celebrities, such as city council members or familiar faces in the media, will be serving up the evening meal.

During your annual event, be sure to tell attendees: "If you enjoyed this evening, wait until you see what we've got in store for you for next year!"

## 4. Key Tools for Event Publicity

The challenge for small nonprofits and membership organizations, according to Lori Halley, a blogger for Wild Apricot (Toronto, Ontario,Canada), is the need for low-cost event publicity ideas.

Starting early and planning ahead will help small organizations with limited resources publicize their events effectively, says Halley.

Among the tools she mentions for maximizing the benefit of event publicity are:

- **Press Release** — necessity for drawing attention to your event. Succinctly offering the who, what, where, when, why and how draws media interest and attention to your event.

- **Media Advisory** — a communication inviting the media to attend your event. The advisory should contain all of the details outlined in your press release and convey a personal welcome extended to members of the media.

- **Media Alert** — a message sent the week prior to the event which reiterates all relevant details one last time.

- **Backgrounder** — a fact sheet with all the event information and pertinent details about your organization. Background information will assist media members in rounding out their coverage of your event.

- **Media Table** — a table at your event where participants and members of the media can find press kits containing the event program, backgrounder, press release, speaker bios, photos and any other collateral materials.

*Source: Lori Halley, Wild Apricot Marketing Writer and Blogger, Wild Apricot/Bonasource Inc., Toronto, Ontario, Canada. Phone (416) 410-4059. E-mail: lori@wildapricot.com. Website: www.wildapricot.com*

### Reach Out to Growing Areas of Your Community

Is your community becoming more culturally diverse? If so, are you stepping up PR methods accordingly? Say that your community has growing numbers of Hispanics and Asians. Bring in representatives of such communities at all stages of event planning -- from coming up with ideas that would appeal to persons of other cultures, to help reaching other cultures through newspapers, churches, social groups and other means.

### Promotion Idea

Invite a reporter to shadow you behind the scenes as you plan the event from start to finish for a feature on the unimaginable amount of work that goes into a charity event. Pitch a business story that profiles local event planners — including yourself — and their most challenging work.

ADMIT ONE

## 5. Create Event Flyers That Pop

Producing eye-catching event flyers is still one of the most cost-effective ways to advertise your event. Flyers need not be complicated; a few unique aspects can have your flyer drawing lots of attention. Try these tips when creating your next event flyer:

❑ Create a flyer unique in size and shape. Cut flyers into shapes such as stars for a dramatic impact. Go with a larger-than-standard size, thinking beyond 8 1/2 x 11 inches.

  ❑ Get your complete message on the flyer, but allow for white space, which lets the reader absorb the information with ease without feeling inundated with details.

  ❑ Use clean, easy-to-read fonts in a large point size for easy readability.

  ❑ Don't forget the details. Include the who, what, when, where, why and how of your event.

  ❑ Align flyer images, shape and style with other print advertising to develop a common theme and recognition for your event.

  ❑ Post flyers throughout your region the week prior to the event. This effort, along with other publicity, creates a double dose of advertising sure to draw guests.

---

### Promotion Idea

Utilize street light banners to promote events around your facility or throughout your community. Get businesses to sponsor banner costs, so they can be used over and over again.

**ADMIT ONE**

---

## 6. 19th Hole Reception Lets Non-golfers Support Cause

Golf tourneys are everywhere, and for a good reason: They're popular ways to raise funds for a cause you support.

But what if you're not a golfer?

The Whitney M. Young, Jr. Foundation's (Albany, NY) 19th Hole Reception offers participants an opportunity to network and support the foundation at an affordable price.

Takara Wiles, development and marketing associate, says the price point was key in their decision to offer the reception-only option.

"We recognize that many people/organizations have cut their budget for activities like golf events since the per-person cost is generally higher than traditional fundraisers (galas, dinners, etc.)," Wiles says. "We also didn't want to exclude supporters of Whitney Young who are not golfers."

The reception-only ticket price is $75 and includes a one-hour open bar and a stationed dinner. A brief awards ceremony recognizes various winners from the tournament itself and raffle winners.

Wiles says the real winner is the foundation, as the event reaches an audience who might have otherwise gone untapped because of their lack of golf prowess or interest. The reception, Wiles says, "is a way for us to spread Whitney Young's mission for those who are unfamiliar with our organization and an opportunity for the non-golfer to support us."

*Source: Takara Wiles, Development and Marketing Associate, Whitney M. Young, Jr. Foundation, Albany, NY. Phone (518) 591-4472. E-mail: twiles@wmyhealth.org*

---

### Spoon Feed Media Pre-event Stories

Check your event itinerary for story ideas to present to the local news media to boost pre-event publicity. Think beyond a predictable phone interview with your keynote speaker or an event preview with your committee chairperson. How about spending an afternoon with the chef who will prepare the decadent dessert buffet for 1,000 guests? Sitting in on a training session for volunteers who will be timing the marathon runners? Even a feature photo in your newspaper or video on the local news showing behind-the-scenes preparations just days before your event can help generate last-minute interest and ticket sales.

## 7. Combine Old Tricks, New Innovations for Success

Earlier this year the Jackson County Court Appointed Special Advocates (Kansas City, MO), which trains volunteers to work as court appointed advocates to underprivileged minors, set a record by holding the largest fundraising breakfast in Kansas City history. Nearly 1,100 guests attended for a chance to hear the organization's members speak about their work helping abused and neglected children.

The event grew from 825 guests in 2010, according to Martha Gershun, executive director of the Jackson County CASA — a 30 percent increase. Gershun was informed by management at Kansas City's Hyatt Regency Crown Center, where CASA's Light of Hope breakfast is traditionally held, that the 2011 event had broken all previous records.

Besides having more attendees than any other fundraising breakfast in the city, CASA raised $145,000 in pre-event sponsorships and day-of donations, says Gershun, who attributes the 2011 breakfast's success to a combination of tried-and-true tricks and a willingness to try out new ways of doing things.

**Promotion Idea**
Host a contest to come up with a theme for this year's event.

**Old Tricks:**

✓ **Don't charge guests to attend.** "That's what works about this event," says Gershun. Instead of asking guests to buy a ticket or pay a door charge, "we recruit table captains who invite their friends to attend and learn more about the agency. We do not charge table captains or their guests. Then we make a direct ask for donations during the event."

✓ **Skip the add-ons.** There are no silent auctions, pledge cards or any other kind of additional revenue streams, says Gershun. "We just tell people about our great work. We have envelopes at every seat, and we walk around and collect the money in baskets at the end of breakfast."

✓ **Stick with a program that works.** The content of the event — showcasing a few inspirational speakers, such as a volunteer or a family that's been helped by CASA — was "exactly what we have done for many years," says Gershun. "Our regular supporters appreciate the predictability of our event."

✓ **Start and end on time!** "The event is exactly one hour, and we never, ever go over that," insists Gershun. "We feel that our busy, professional supporters appreciate that we respect their time. One of the primary compliments I hear about the event is, 'You always end on time!'"

**New Tricks:**

✓ **Promote through social media.** This year, for the first time, the Light of Hope breakfast's publicity included "a strong Facebook presence, electronic invitations and e-mail pushes," says Gershun. In fact, she says that starting next year, "I don't think we will spend any money on printing and mailing invitations or save-the-date cards — I think we can do everything electronically."

✓ **Ask your volunteers to help recruit donors.** This was another change from years past. "Historically we have felt that we shouldn't ask our volunteers to help with fundraising, but we found that they like to use this event to share their CASA work with their friends, family members and colleagues," Gershun says.

*Source: Martha Gershun, Executive Director, Jackson County Court Appointed Special Advocates, Kansas City, MO. Phone (816) 984-8208.*
*E-mail: mgershun@jacksoncountycasa-mo.org. Website: www.jacksoncountycasa-mo.org*

## 8. Attract New Attendees

*Q.* *"How do you reach out to new event attendees?"*

"Each year we host a fundraising dinner where we bestow awards to four honorees. One way we interest new people in the event is by gathering names from the honorees of their friends and colleagues who would enjoy being invited. Secondly, we solicit names and addresses from our board of directors as well as host committee members. Finally, we gather the names of guests invited by our many table sponsors. During the event, we provide opportunities for people new to the organization to be on our mailing/e-mail lists for further information."

— *Sandra L. DeSobe, Psychotherapist,*
*Krist Samaritan Center for Counseling and Education (Houston, TX)*

"Three years ago we began advertising in two Hispanic magazines for our annual Boo at the Zoo event. This has led to a special one-night feature of Boo to celebrate 'el Dia de los Muertos' (Day of the Dead), which is Hispanic Halloween. One night a stage is set up with authentic decorations, music, activities and performers. This greatly increased the number of Hispanic guests at our event.

"We have also advertised with the chamber of commerce, any publication that is delivered to new residents in our community and with local realtors."

— *Zetta Friday, Special Events Coordinator, Little Rock Zoo (Little Rock, AR)*

### Promotion Idea

Have your UPS or FedEx delivery person hand out flyers promoting the event to everyone on their route, asking businesses to display the flyers in their windows.

**ADMIT ONE**

## 9. Involve Board Members in Your Special Events

Whether coordinating an awareness walk, black-tie gala or chili cook-off championship, there's value in getting board members involved in your special events.

Although other volunteers may be heavily committed to planning and executing an event, be sure your board has some responsibility for carrying off a successful fundraiser. Ask each board member, for instance, to sell a minimum number of tickets or enlist a set number of sponsors.

Most importantly, convey the importance of their presence at your event. Provide them with distinctive badges that separate them from all others.

In promoting board member involvement, keep in mind their presence at events:

- Helps strengthen board ownership of the organization.

- Provides board members with a better understanding of how such events fit into the overall development plan.

- Gives board members the opportunity to act as ambassadors on your cause's behalf.

- Allows your board to experience a more festive and fun aspect of your organization.

## 10. Advertise as Early and Often as Possible

Face it. While many folks plan their social schedules weeks or even months in advance, more people than ever make last-minute decisions. That's why it's important to get the word out about your event as early and late and often as possible.

Look for ways to generate additional press beyond the initial press release. Only five days left to get in on discounted tickets? Send a paragraph-long reminder to local news media. Will your development director speak about the event at a local service group meeting? Send a paragraph about the fact to the media, noting that he/she will be open to questions from the media at the event. Hit the news media up the week or day prior to your event to give 15 seconds of airtime or three lines of editorial copy to the fact that your event is fast approaching, and that people can buy tickets up to and during the event itself.

## 11. Draw Attendance, Attention With Well-designed Event Posters

The more attractive and eye-catching your event poster is, the more likely people will be to display it, notice it and want to find out more about your special event. Exceptional designs may even turn into collectible art, with supporters looking forward to your design each year, as with posters promoting jazz festivals in Monterey and New Orleans.

Here are some tips for inspiring your creativity:

✓ **Look at art books.** Books with examples of effective poster designs are a gold mine of ideas and how-to tips, and may include background about why the designs worked so well.

✓ **Realize brief copy enhances design.** Date, time, place, purpose and contact information are usually all you need, leaving space for bold art and pleasing layout.

✓ **Place yard signs where posters cannot go.** Well-done yard signs can go outside stores, in volunteers' yards and on busy street corners. Keep graphics and details bold so motorists can see them and remember at least enough to know where to buy tickets.

✓ **Use attractive, unusual fonts.** When budget prohibits purchasing art or contracting with an artist, let artistic typography tell your story. Use positive and negative backgrounds and shapes to highlight details. Think of American sculptor Alexander Calder's mobiles (www.calder.org) and translate the concept to paper.

✓ **Consider ingenious display strategies.** Laminate posters on foam board and hang from ceilings on sturdy string to be visible from both sides or displayed on an easel on counter tops in public areas. Leave extra copies for standard wall and window display.

✓ **Try window clings and magnet posters.** Ordered in large enough quantity, both can be cost effective. Larger formats cost more, but may be useful for select locations.

**ADMIT ONE**

### Promotion Idea

Create a poster contest for your event open to the youth of your community. Ask them to design a poster based on this year's event theme. The winning poster could be reproduced and used to promote the event.

## 12. How to Increase Ticket Sales by 30 Percent

If your goal is to raise more money with your special event, you can either raise the ticket price or attract more guests. Either way, you need to make sure tickets get sold.

Begin by doing the math. Assuming your ticket price is set, let's say you want to increase ticket sales by 30 percent over last year. So if 200 people attended last year's event, that's 60 more tickets that need to be sold.

Knowing board members and volunteers play a key role in selling tickets, consider any of these strategies as a way to boost ticket sales significantly:

- Ask 50 of the previous year's most loyal attendees to each sell two tickets.
- Offer donated prizes (Netbook, iPod, restaurant gift certificate) for most tickets sold.
- Offer a lesser prize (signed book, Starbucks gift cards) to anyone who sells a minimum number of tickets.
- Extend an invitation for your employees to sell tickets and attend the event for free or at a reduced rate as a way to thank them.

## 13. Enhance Your Event's Approachability Factor

Increase your event's approachability factor by painting a clear picture of what potential attendees should expect. Be specific. Use detailed descriptions about the theme, decor, intended audience, dress expectations and other factors of your event's ambiance.

Depending on your event type, consider phrases such as these for invitations and advertising materials:

- Don your Saturday-night finest for this exclusive black-tie soiree; Photography by Kate will be on hand to take keepsake glamour shots of couples, groups and individuals.
- Grab a blanket, lawn chairs, the kids, the neighbors and the dog for a great afternoon of free music! (Please remember Clancy Park's no alcohol, no-cooler policy. We'll have free lemonade and ice cream for everyone, and pizza and barbecue vendors will be on site selling other foods and refreshments.)
- Costumes optional for our Mardi Gras ball — come dressed for dancing and we'll provide the beads and colorful masks!
- You won't want to miss our keynote speaker, sure to bring laughs galore with his G-rated comedy act!
- Whether you're out to set a new world's record or for a relaxing stroll, our annual run/walk is the place to be for all ages! Timed events begin at 9 a.m., followed by the all-community riverfront stroll (definitely not timed!) at 10 a.m. Strollers, wagons, wheelchairs and adult scooters welcome. Please remember the riverfront's no-skateboard, no-rollerblade, no-bicycle rule and leave those wheels at home.

**Promotion Idea**

Host a radiothon to help spread the word. Ask radio stations to do a live remote from your event.

ADMIT ONE

## 14. Go All Out on Publicity Materials

Don't settle for good enough when creating invitations, flyers and posters. Wow 'em with marketing materials that capture the spirit and fun of the event.

Create a logo that people immediately connect with your special event, and use and reuse it throughout the community. For example, for its popular annual riverfront art fair and celebration, one Midwest community calls on a locally based, nationally recognized artist to design a colorful, free-spirited poster advertising the two-day event.

Since the artist comes up with a new idea for each year, the posters are in demand, not only to advertise the riverfront art celebration, but to frame and display for years to come.

**ADMIT ONE**

### Promotion Idea

Prepare a publicity checklist to ensure no promotional ideas are left on the table. Share it with everyone involved with planning your event.

## 15. Press Releases That Get Your Event Noticed

Getting the word out about your special event is one of the most important aspects of the planning process. You may have the greatest event ever, but if no one hears about it, no one will come.

The most cost-efficient way to publicize your event is with a press release to the local media. But while you're sending in your finely crafted press release, so are many other nonprofits. Making your release stand out from all the others will insure it gets published on time and may catch the attention of a reporter for a feature story.

Here are some tips to make sure your press release gets the attention it deserves:

- **Use a style guide.** Some publications use an in-house style guide, but most follow the basic rules set forth in guide books such as the Associated Press Stylebook. If your release is written in the same style as the publication, busy journalists rushing to meet a deadline will not have to rewrite it.

- **Write the release to match the purpose.** If you're writing a release for the community calendar portion of the newspaper, write it in the style of the calendar listing, not a full release. Keep it extremely brief and include only the necessary facts. A notice sent to a radio or TV station to be read as a public service announcement (PSA) should also be an abbreviated version of the full release.

- **Develop a style sheet of your own.** Having an in-house style sheet for your organization will help answer questions such as: What's the correct tag line to describe the organization? Must board member names be included in every release? What phone number or extension should be listed in news stories? Who is the designated press contact? What acronyms need to be explained?

By having your own style sheet, each press release will look the same, no matter who writes it.

### Attendance-busting Ideas

To increase attendance for your event, come up with a way to get on the evening news the week of your event. To do that, come up with an attention-grabbing hook that local stations will want to carry.

Consider any of these ideas:

✓ Showcase a handful of individuals who will benefit from the funds being raised.

✓ If it's a themed event, enlist two or three people to be interviewed in costume.

✓ Share the name(s) of any celebrities who will be in attendance.

✓ Announce the chance for attendees to win a major prize.

## 16. Don't Skimp on Advertising or Marketing

Think you've hit all possible venues to get the word out about your event? Think again. Beyond the obvious local TV, radio and newspapers, consider sending news releases, bundles of take-home flyers and/or posters touting your big event to:

- Area churches and synagogues
- Colleges and technical schools
- Public libraries
- Service clubs, organizations
- Newspapers for area minorities
- Area businesses' employee newsletters
- Daycares, preschools, K-12
- Area restaurants and bars
- Grocery stores, shopping malls
- Craft stores, quilting stores
- All of your sponsors

## 17. Link to Social Media Networks

In today's technologically savvy world, tweeting isn't just for the birds.

Even members of Congress use social media like Twitter.com to stay in touch with constituents in real time, sending brief text messages (called tweeting) that can be viewed on the Internet, cell phones and other portable communications devices.

Facebook (www.facebook.com), LinkedIn (www.linkedin.com), Flickr (www.flickr.com) and YouTube (www.youtube.com) are just a few of the free online social media sites where you can create an account or group to communicate with existing volunteers and recruit new ones.

To put these social networking tools to use promoting your special event, increase your organization's online presence and boost awareness of your mission:

- ❑ **Start a Facebook group about your event.** Once you have recruited or identified supporters who already use Facebook, you can send invitations to meetings, post photo albums, give daily progress reports about completed tasks and reservations and advertise jobs that still need to be done.

- ❑ **Twitter messages to spread news.** Your committee meeting has been canceled, but you can't call everyone in time. Twitter allows you to log on to your account and spread the word to many users at once, who can, in turn, notify others of the change in plans.

- ❑ **Launch a photo album and blog on Flickr.** Some of your volunteers have traveled to Africa on behalf of your organization. Start an account where they can post photos, write about their activities and share links to news with those at home.

- ❑ **Study social media options for the best fit.** Chances are that many of your volunteers already have accounts on LinkedIn, Twitter, Facebook, YouTube or Flickr. Most of these sites link to each other, so news you share can have a positive ripple effect. Portal websites, like www.socialmediaanswers.com, give tutorials on how to build and cultivate your own network, and describe the benefits of the most popular and versatile services.

### Promotion Idea

Contact your local chamber of commerce to get your event on their calendar and ask them to send your event flyer with their regularly published newsletter.

ADMIT ONE

## 18. Make the Most of a Volunteer Publicity Committee

As you evaluate the publicity needs for your special event, evaluate your volunteer corps as well. Do you have volunteers whose background or talents are a good match for a specific type of publicity?

Even in large organizations, it's most effective to think small when recruiting volunteers to serve on your publicity committee. One well-rounded and experienced individual, accompanied by an assistant chairperson, may be more than adequate for some events.

If your major event or slate of several upcoming events will require more extensive publicity efforts, think first of the categories of coverage you hope to attract:

**ADMIT ONE**

**Promotion Idea**

Be sure to have a publicity and media relations committee to give publicity the constant and creative attention it deserves. Consider including members of the press on your committee.

- **Television, radio and newspapers.** Public service announcements, press releases and photographs are among the most useful vehicles for informing the community of your events. A person who writes news releases well and can draft copy for radio announcements will be a valuable addition to your committee. Even if the volunteer has never had professional experience in these areas, possessing the skill to write concise facts for editors and producers will be appreciated.

- **Your organization's ambassador.** Every organization has an individual who has friends and contacts to enlist to help your cause. This person may have excellent telephone skills and be diligent about follow-up calls to media or sponsors who have agreed to help you with publicity. A community liaison with broad-based knowledge of publicity resources should be the primary contact for media and will help avoid duplicate calls to others on the committee.

- **Attractive presentation of publicity proposals.** Once you have found individuals who can communicate well both on paper and in person, a designer, decorator or artistic person can round out the group. The combination of well-written facts, attractive graphics for printed materials or promotional posters, and a pleasant presentation to media representatives will help your organization stand above those who simply call or mail news releases.

### Coordinating Internal and External Publicity

Go beyond matching volunteers to publicity tasks, as detailed above, to make sure your employees know details of special events as well.

When paid staff produce newsletters and brochures for activities, involve them in the volunteer efforts to increase the impact of your combined efforts. Both paid staff and volunteers bring expertise to the table, while a volunteer may have a more flexible schedule to meet with media at the media's convenience. By the same token, one of your paid staff may have professional media contacts who would be willing to work with your organization's volunteer.

Look at all resources within your organization, whether they are offered by volunteers or staff. Pair them when the combination of skills and chemistry is logical to save time and increase creative energy.

Have a clear description of duties for each member of the publicity committee so each member knows what he/she should pursue, and what his/her fellow committee members are doing. Should they decide between themselves that one is better suited than the others for a specific duty, allow for flexibility in achieving the publicity objective as long as everyone is agreeable.

Your involvement is important to them as a resource and guide, but if you have asked the best-qualified persons to serve, all you will really need are regular updates on their progress, and to be sure they have the support they need from other volunteers and staff.

## 19. Encourage Event Buy-in to Boost Attendance

Want super attendance at your next event? Offer opportunities for the public to become involved without having to play a key role.

Here are a few examples of ways to involve the public and draw them to attend an event:

- Create a contest to name the event. Publicize and reward the winner.
- Ask key persons to be present by virtue of their positions: elected officials, media representatives, local celebrities, etc.
- Name honorary guests, chairpersons or awards recipients who will enjoy the limelight.
- Involve a performance by youth that will bring their parents to the event.
- Host an exhibit of people's artwork, photographs or crafts to draw their presence.

Any and all linkages you can create between people and your event will enhance their desire to attend it.

## 20. Use Creativity When Designing Event Invitations

Invitations to your organization's events need not be costly to be effective or memorable. Let these ideas get you started and inspire your creative team:

- ❑ **Business-card-sized invitations**. The who, what, when, where and why of most events can fit on a blank printable business card, especially if the event is open to the public and formal mailing lists aren't needed. Leave stacks at businesses, distribute at networking events and have volunteers hand them out.

- ❑ **Carefully evaluate needs**. Will your invitation design have equal impact with just one or two colors? A well-executed graphic and attractive layout can look great in black or grayscale and cost less than more colorful versions.

- ❑ **Stick it!** Shop the marketplace for bright adhesive stickers in interesting shapes, and design your basic invitation to accommodate them in the design theme. Besides using them on the invitation, add them to the mailing envelope and response cards.

- ❑ **Use surplus materials in your inventory**. Take a tip from Scarlett O'Hara, who made a gown from drapes. Leftover blank envelopes and outdated letterhead trimmed to size can be a blank canvas for your invitation.

- ❑ **Plantable, printable paper**. Seeded papers, party favors, place cards and even confetti are available from online retailers and specialty stores. When planted, they grow into flowers.

- ❑ **Look online for ready-made cards**. Sourcing artwork and design on invitation websites helps you obtain professional-looking results and saves money and time. Dozens of online retailers offer broad selections of stock images with themes for total invitation packages that are printed and shipped within a week or two. Some also will provide matching artwork for e-cards.

- ❑ **Vary materials**. Consider integrating into your invitation a swatch of colorful fabric, unique twine, die-cut flower or other shape, spiced tea bag or other small items that fit your event theme. They can add color, interest and context when appropriately used.

---

**Promotion Idea**

Print event posters on 4 X 6 inch sheets and ask your local supermarket to stuff posters in bags at the checkout.

ADMIT ONE

---

**Go 3D With Invitations**

To make invitations more eye-catching, make them three dimensional by attaching an item to the front panel: a square inch of cloth, a snippet of evergreen or an appropriate item tied to the invitation with ribbon.

---

## 21. Consider the Benefits of Partnering For Special Events

Have you ever used a special event as a chance to collaborate with another charity?

Special events offer tremendous opportunities for creating partnerships. Such partnerships can be with another nonprofit that has similar interests and goals or with a group completely different from your own. Each has its own benefits. For example:

❑ **Collaborating with a similar organization.** If your organization is involved with health care, for example, you could partner with similar groups to have a large health fair event. The advantage: The groups could share the cost and work involved with the event as well as share in the realized profits.

❑ **Partnering with an organization unlike your own.** You could partner with a group totally unrelated to your cause, such as a health care group joining forces with a museum, and then billing it as an event to benefit two worthwhile charitable organizations. The advantage: Each organization would expose its cause to a whole new group of potential donors and volunteers.

> **ADMIT ONE**
>
> **Promotion Idea**
>
> Recruit a local media sponsor who can exchange advertising space or time for sponsorship identification. Make sure to gain sponsors from the main media categories — print, radio and television — to maximize your in-kind advertising exposure.

## 22. Prestigious Location Keeps Golfers Coming Back

The chance to play on the course where Tiger Woods won the 1995 United States Amateur Tournament might seem like enough of a draw for a fundraising golf tourney. Indeed, that location — the Newport Country Club (Newport, RI) — is the most appealing aspect of the President's Cup Golf Tournament hosted by Bryant University (Smithfield, RI), says Assistant Director of Annual Giving John Garcia.

"The Newport Country Club is a private club with a rich history, including playing host to PGA tour events," Garcia says. "This helps us sell out the event each year."

While the location may be the draw, the most rewarding part of the day is raising scholarship money for the President's Scholarship Fund at Bryant, says Garcia.

Two levels of foursomes allow golfers and sponsors to choose between a straight foursome at $3,000, or a $5,000 scholarship sponsor contribution, which includes a foursome, invitation to the live/silent auction reception, a tee sign, a pin flag that flies all day and a framed pin flag presented to the sponsor. Non-golfing sponsorships range from a $500 pin flag to a dinner sponsorship at $7,500.

For $20, the Buy-A-Drive hole feature allows golfers to buy a drive from one of Bryant's student golfers who volunteer at the event. Both the student golfer and tournament golfer tee off, with the option to play the best drive. Golfers also choose from gift packages that include items such as golf shoes, clubs and golf balls. Each golfer also receives a hole favor at each hole, such as a polo shirt, necktie or lunch cooler.

All proceeds from the tournament support the President's Scholarship Fund at Bryant. Since its inception, the tournament has raised nearly $519,000.

> **Pre-event Publicity**
>
> Here is one way to garner some pre-event publicity for your next golf event: About two weeks prior to your golf classic, host a shot in the dark evening competition for committee members and media invites. Assemble at a golf course and give each attendee a one-time swing at one of the shorter holes. The person who comes closest to the hole in one shot — if you can locate everyone's ball in the dark — wins a donated prize. Refreshments can be served prior to or following the competition.

*Source: John Garcia, Assistant Director of Annual Giving, Bryant University, Smithfield, RI. Phone (401) 232-6557. E-mail: jgarcia@bryant.edu.*
*Website: www.bryant.edu/presidentscupgolf*

## 23. Solicit Artwork and Artists, Families Will Come

Ask for artwork related to your cause, such as a child's drawing showing how your hospital made a difference to their family, or photos from the nature preserve your nonprofit works to keep clean. Make room at your special event to display all entries. Set the art submission deadline two weeks before your event, then send out invitations to all persons who sent in entries to purchase tickets and attend.

## 24. Start Off on the Right Foot With Show-stopping Invitations

With nearly everyone's mailboxes and e-mail in-boxes overloaded, make sure your event invitations get noticed with these creative approaches or delivery methods:

- ✓ **Frame it up.** Send your one-sided invitation in a colorful standard-size photo frame that can be customized to fit your theme and become a collectible souvenir for annual events. Buy in bulk for consistency and savings.

- ✓ **Offer the sweet smell of success.** Choose a scented or scratch-and-sniff paper with a fragrance to match the event, like pineapple for a luau or peppermint for an ice cream social. Scented oils dabbed on standard paper also suffice.

- ✓ **Invite and advertise.** Design and print T-shirts with event details. If the to-do is open to the public, have persons wear shirts in advance to encourage ticket sales.

- ✓ **Send candy.** Search online or through local party stores for chocolate bars, large cookies and treat tins that can be personalized to spell out event details.

- ✓ **E-mail a PDF or image file.** Instead of paper and postage, use your budget for colorful graphic design that pops right off the monitor and is suitable as a screen saver. When links to your web page are included, you can go into much more detail about the event than in a traditional invitation, and get RSVPs online.

- ✓ **Broadcast yourself.** Create a short and entertaining YouTube video promoting your celebration with the most talented singers or dancers you can find, sending the URL to your e-mail database and linking it to your website. Brainstorm a clever subject line to make recipients open their e-mail.

- ✓ **Make it charming.** While confetti or sprinkles falling out of an envelope may annoy some, a small charm, ornate button or bow, lace trim or tiny toy attached to the paper will add dimension and personality to an otherwise standard design.

- ✓ **Look for online templates and adaptable designs.** The Internet is a limitless source of free design templates for creating your own invitation, as well as samples of ready-made papers, sets and themes that can be personalized with font choices and colors. Allow adequate time for online proofing, printing and delivery to your facility, and addressing and mailing at least three weeks prior to the event.

- ✓ **Try artistic photo treatments.** Use a photo of an event speaker or honoree engaging in an activity fitting your theme. Photo editing programs can turn it into a colorful drawing with a whimsical background, or even put your subject on the cover of a famous magazine or newspaper where your event details are the lead story.

---

**Promotion Idea**

Create displays on your campus and at key community businesses that grab passersby.

ADMIT ONE

---

## 25. Create Buzz for Your Next Event and Watch Attendance Soar

What can you do to make your event the must-attend affair in your community — the one with the wow factor? Here are a few drawing cards you could announce as the build up to your event:

✓ A local/national/international celebrity will attend (and possibly play a key role).

✓ An important announcement of positive community impact will be made.

✓ Some form of celebrated entertainment will be provided.

✓ Every attendee will be eligible to win a fantastic prize.

✓ The event will feature the unveiling of a much-anticipated feature/service/artwork.

## 26. To Get Celebrities to Your Event, Challenge Them

Finagling somebody famous to appear at your fundraising event can require endless time, effort and patience — and oftentimes, you still end up with a no.

Turn the tables by issuing a public challenge to the celebrities you want to show up. Then sit back and watch as they work to meet that challenge!

That's what organizers of Hoops for Hope LA accomplished with a onetime celebrity basketball fundraiser held in February at Staples Center (Los Angeles, CA).

Officials with two nonprofit groups collaborated in creating the event: The Arnold C. Yoder Survivors Foundation (Beverly Hills, CA), which offers therapy and support to children and families coping with grief, and Hawks Hoops Sports Foundation (Long Beach, CA), dedicated to providing youth mentoring and basketball programming throughout the area.

With less than a month to organize the event, former NBA player and event co-planner Juaquin Hawkins, president of Hawks Hoops, turned to social media outlets such as Facebook, YouTube and Twitter. Through postings, tweets and videos, Hawkins directly addressed a number of sports and entertainment stars in the LA area, including Magic Johnson, challenging them to appear at Hoops for Hope.

Even a standard press release issued about the challenge encouraged participation with the words: "We are asking everyone who views this news release to send out the official tweet!"

Hollywood set the trend of relying on social media for free publicity, so the result was a turnout of celebrities so large that a line-up of musical acts, including the Billboard-charting Cali Swag District, performed at the event in addition to the scheduled basketball game. An on-site celebrity phone bank was streamed live on the Internet for those who could not attend but wanted to contribute through a telethon.

Hawkins says one major benefit of issuing a celebrity challenge is that the hours you put into it double as free publicity for the event and for your organization.

*Source: Juaquin Hawkins, President, Hawks Hoops Sports Foundation, Long Beach, CA. Phone (562) 318-7044. E-mail: hawkhoopscamp@aol.com. Website: www.hawk-hoops.com*

**ADMIT ONE**

**Promotion Idea**

Use well-known honorees and civic or industry leaders who can help put a face to your cause and benefit your event.

## 27. Host a Traffic-generating Contest

Competition always helps generate interest. Keep the category fun and fresh and you'll make everyone happy, regardless of who is named winner.
For example:

- Oldest/smelliest/most-mileage shoes
- Pet/owner look-alike contest
- Spelling bee for adults
- Dirtiest vehicle competition
- Best homemade salsa
- Photo contest showing library patrons reading
- Singing/karaoke contest

### Promotion Idea

Host a photo contest on your organization's website asking people to submit photos of themselves that may be related to your event (e.g., pet/owner look-alike contest).

**ADMIT ONE**

## 28. Make Events More Accessible

What can you do to make your event more accessible to individuals with special needs?

Danny Kodmur, disability access specialist at the University of California, Berkeley (Berkeley, CA), regularly offers advice and guidance on how to make events more accessible. Here, he shares seven tips for making your next event more accessible to people with disabilities:

1. Have an access request process and mention it in all event publicity. Identify an access point person on staff as the publicity contact. Give a timeline for making requests, but be aware you'll need to make a good-faith effort to accommodate requests regardless of when you receive them.

2. Know your event venue, and collect/disseminate its access information appropriately (e.g., list accessible parking/restrooms/paths of travel/elevator locations, etc.). Post signage on event day.

3. Know that you may have attendees who do not identify themselves as disabled or use your access request process, but who may still have significant mobility and/or communication needs.

4. Be mindful not to isolate people who use wheelchairs. Choose facilities with rooms that allow placement of wheelchairs within the main seating area of the room.

5. Work in advance to provide alternative media for visually impaired attendees; prepare written materials and outlines for sign language interpreters or real-time captioners, well in advance. When possible, create closed-captions all media shown at the event.

6. Access is a necessity, not a frill. Make accessibility costs part of your overall event overhead, including fees for interpreters and captioners.

7. If your event has access limitations that you can't do anything about, communicate the limitations to potential attendees. That way, persons with disabilities can make decisions about whether or how to attend an event with problematic access based upon accurate information.

*Source: Danny Kodmur, Disability Access Specialist, Disability Access Services, University of California, Berkeley, Berkeley, CA. Phone (510) 643-6456. Website: http://access.berkeley.edu*

### Include Testimonials When Promoting Annual Events

Here's an added feature when publicizing annual events: Include testimonials from a variety of past attendees — the more well-known the better.

Not only will their comments attract others, those who share their views will be more likely to attend since they backed the event. It's a way to involve people that won't take that much time.

## 29. Marketing Efforts Bring Home the Bacon

Organizers of Baconfest (Chicago, IL) credit its growing popularity to strong marketing efforts that include a consistent Facebook presence, frequent Twitter posts and mini-features at the event website, www.baconfestchicago.com.

Mini-features are written or videotaped pieces that elaborate on a specific event element. Mini-features for 2011 included a story on the event's official beverage, an article on exhibiting restaurants, the support of the Illinois Pork Producers and announcement of the 2011 Bacon Poetry contest.

Michael Griggs, event co-founder, shares ideas for mini-features to keep your event in the news:

- **Work on your voice.** "We spend a lot of energy making sure that the voice of Baconfest is fun, informal and engaging. The web is an informal medium and traditional press release voicing doesn't make sense for content designed to be consumed by your customers directly."

- **Keep it short.** A maximum of 500 words for a written article and three minutes maximum for a video if recommended.

- **Use all your communications channels.** Each new piece of content gives you a new opportunity to remind supporters that you exist.

- **Build media relationships.** "We work to keep up personal relationships with food media and bloggers in Chicago; those are the people who will spread the word about what we're doing most effectively."

*Source: Michael Griggs, Co-founder, Baconfest, Chicago, IL. Phone (773) 257-3378. E-mail: michael@baconfestchicago.com. Website: www.baconfestchicago.com*

> **ADMIT ONE**
>
> **Promotion Idea**
>
> If your event includes gourmet or special food delights, wet peoples' appetites by doing pre-event demonstrations or media appearances about various aspects of the food preparation.

## 30. Market Special Events With New Mobile Application

Foursquare (www.foursquare.com) — a new mobile application similar to Twitter (www.twitter.com) — offers ways to market special events or recruit volunteers.

Foursquare is designed to simplify exploring cities for users. Users check in to report their current whereabouts and post shoutouts to let friends know why they like a certain place. In turn, they rely on Foursquare to find nearby friends and get first-person impressions on new places.

To get attention on Foursquare:

- Add your nonprofit as a listing in your city on Foursquare to allow users to find it, learn ways to volunteer or be aware of events to attend that boost your cause.

- Become a user. Start using Foursquare to learn how it might benefit your nonprofit. As you become more proficient with using Foursquare, add tips about your nonprofit, including details on upcoming events.

- Develop camaraderie. Create an event specifically for Foursquare users at your nonprofit. Host a meet and greet or service event for Foursquare users in your area to solidify your corner of Foursquare.

> **Benefits of Collaboration**
>
> If you're finding it tough to attract people to special events in these economic times, try this: Partner with a dissimilar nonprofit on a joint fundraising event. By partnering and splitting the profit, you can also:
>
> - Cut expenses in half.
> - Attract twice as many guests.
> - Share planning responsibilities.
> - Make friends with potential donors.
> - Make a positive statement about cooperation between two worthy causes.

## 31. Timing Impacts Attendance

You recently launched a new fundraising event, and while feedback was positive, attendance was lackluster. Why? Perhaps it was your timing.

When scheduling your event, check the community calendar well in advance. Perhaps another agency has decided to launch a similar event a week or two earlier or even the same week or day. For effective attendance, be sure to allow at least 30 days between event launches.

Also, be sure to advertise your event well ahead of time. Perform three or four communications approximately 30 days before each event. Don't forget official news publication notices, member e-mail announcements, short radio spots and a reminder e-mail to all agency members and attendees.

Finally, don't assume you've ever done enough or explored enough alternative channels to communicate your event. Always investigate new avenues.

## 32. Attracting People to Events

The Girl Scouts' song lyrics, "Make new friends, but keep the old; one is silver and the other gold," can apply to attracting newcomers to your organization's special events and volunteer base.

Consider several of these tips to bring in fresh faces while also retaining your loyal supporters:

- ❑ **Host a Friends and Family Day.** If you haven't sponsored a broad-appeal event suitable for all ages and incomes, do so with the specific purpose of increasing awareness of your programs. Include entertaining activities, demonstrations, tours and refreshments. Be sure to specifically ask existing volunteers and staff to bring their friends and relatives.

- ❑ **Bring in a unique guest speaker.** Research issues that fit within your scope, but look for new messengers, as well. For example, young audiences may be eager to hear from someone who has returned from a mission to Darfur or spent weeks in New Orleans building new homes for Hurricane Katrina evacuees. Advance news features about the speaker with time and date of the program can draw even more interest.

- ❑ **Reach out to artists and craftsmen.** Art fairs can attract wide audiences. Invite painters, quilters, woodcarvers, potters and the like to display and sell their work with a portion of proceeds going to your organization. Have your organization's representatives staff booths or stations to greet new faces and share information on your cause.

- ❑ **Go bilingual.** If your community has a growing base of Hispanic people or others who are still learning English, produce some of your materials in their language and have bilingual staff or volunteers on hand to tell them about your volunteer opportunities.

- ❑ **Target newcomers.** Work with other agencies that help acquaint newcomers to your service area, so that your materials are included in their welcome packages. Develop a resource brochure that outlines many volunteer opportunities in the community, but highlight your own and those of organizations that may partner with you.

### Promotion Idea

Integrate promotion of an event into a parade. Place signage on antique cars or create your own float that publicizes your upcoming event.

**ADMIT ONE**

## 33. Turn Invite Into Low-cost, High-impact Marketing Tool

Don't know what to do with those old photos? Why not turn them into a collectors' series and use them as invitations to your next event?

Each invitation comes in two detachable parts: a ticket valid for single admission to the event, and a collectible souvenir card featuring an historical person, place or thing.

Select four or five photos of locally famous people, buildings or other landmarks to feature on the cards. Include text about your organization or cause. The key is to give people an incentive to collect the entire series.

You can use this idea for raffle tickets, special event invitations or entrance or performance tickets.

Here are some tips:

1. The card should look like a postcard you'd like to send to a friend or family member. In fact, design the flip side to serve as a postcard.
2. The photo should engage the recipient so they read the text blurb you include on the card and want to find out more.
3. Include your web address in the blurb.

## 34. Get Creative When Seeking Pre-event Publicity

Press releases and media interviews are excellent ways to attract publicity before your special event, but you may need to do more than that to truly grab the spotlight and inspire audiences to attend.

As appropriate, add these elements to your publicity repertoire:

- ❑ Announce changes and additions. Has the sluggish economy caused you to rethink your target audience? Tell the press. If your formal gala is now a festive family celebration with reduced ticket or table prices, that's a human interest story. Be upbeat about providing better value for your supporters and drawing a potentially larger audience.

- ❑ Arrange interviews with honorees. Create a buzz around the people you are honoring at your event. Tell the public why they are worthy of recognition from the entire community. Even those who cannot attend will be more aware of your organization's mission and services and admire those who help make it successful.

- ❑ Invite the public to watch the event. While most people buy tickets to help you reach your goal, look for opportunities or activities spectators can observe free of charge. For example, a competition to hit a hole in one or shoot a basket for a large cash prize or a fireworks show can generate advance media coverage and community interest.

- ❑ Start a fun awareness campaign. A first step might be a billboard or newspaper ad announcing only, "It's coming." Add details once a week like, "It's coming August 8th," and "It's coming August 8th to Community Hospital," until the who, what, when, where and why are fully revealed.

- ❑ Offer free admission to the first 10 (or other such number) people. A famous author is donating and signing books for you. A popular rock band is giving a benefit concert and selling CDs. All signs point to a sellout, but you can generate good will and positive publicity by giving away a few spots to early birds who are fans of your event's star.

**ADMIT ONE**

**Promotion Idea**

If you're counting on coverage in regional, statewide or even national magazines, be sure to know their editorial deadlines in advance.

## 35. Getting Press for Your Event

If you want press coverage of your special event, plan for it. Prepare a detailed media list. Include all local/regional radio and TV stations, newspapers and local magazines. Call everyone on the list to find out to whom your press release should be sent and what the deadlines are. Always speak to a real person, don't just rely on mail or e-mail to get the job done.

Want to have an article run before or after the event? To improve your chances of getting coverage, find an interesting angle. What makes your event newsworthy? Be sure to convey what the proceeds will mean to real people.

Also, don't forget about alternative forms of publicity. Take advantage of any place that will let you post a notice of your event — billboards, motel/church marquees, pamphlets in convenience stores, libraries, store bulletin boards, visitor centers, table displays in restaurants, merchant windows, cable TV community news listings, closed-circuit TV systems at local hotels, etc.

In addition, check to see if your city has a Web page dedicated to charitable or other local events.

## 36. Make Your Website Work for Your Event

Whether you host an event once a year or once a week, realize that potential attendees will turn to your website to learn more.

Officials at Evangelical Community Hospital (Lewisburg, PA) organize an annual Evening of Giving to benefit its hospice program. For $5, attendees shop and receive discounts after regular business hours at their favorite stores at an area mall. On average 1,000 people attend the event, which raises $10,000 to $20,000.

The event website includes information on event time and location, tickets, discounts, door prizes, food sample vendors, special giveaways, raffles, sponsor recognition, photos and logos.

Attendees use the event Web page (www.evanhospital.com/special/Event.aspx?id=11) to decide which stores to visit during the event, and forward it to friends, says Development Assistant Heather Black. "The site also allows for extra publicity for sponsors, who in tough economic times like to know they're getting the most value out of their sponsorship dollars."

Black says they post basic event information several months in advance, and more frequently as the event approaches. After the event, they post dollars raised, prize and raffle winners' names, photos and information on next year's event.

At Children's Museum of Houston (Houston, TX), daily maintenance is required to stay up-to-date on numerous special events. Henry Yau, public relations and promotions director, says viewers can choose to view the online calendar (www.cmhouston.org/en/cev/mon/) in a weekly or monthly view, choosing an event type to quickly learn more about it.

"People want to know what's happening that day," says Yau. "Each day we highlight the biggest event, and that is typically the event that brings in the most money."

The website's events section includes information on smaller events, admission fees, parking and photos of past events. Says Yau, noting, "If people see a photo, they'll be more inclined to come. A picture gives people a clue as to what to expect."

*Sources: Heather Black, Development Assistant, Evangelical Community Hospital, Lewisburg, PA. Phone (570) 522-4850. E-mail: hblack@evanhospital.com*
*Henry Yau, Public Relations and Promotions Director, Children's Museum of Houston, Houston, TX. Phone (713) 535-7267. E-mail: hyau@cmhouston.org*

### Promotion Idea

Ask your event vendors (e.g., band, caterer, etc.) to include event information in their e-mail blasts, calendars and websites.

ADMIT ONE

## 37. Let Them Vote

Create a fun, attention-grabbing contest in which members of your community cast ballots for an all-in-fun contest. Have all contestants attend as special guests of your event, and unveil the top vote-getter during the festivities. Fun contests include the UGLY-est city council member (meaning Understanding, Generous Lovable You!), or the baddest (as in best) DJ or news anchor with the best hidden talent.

## 38. Host a Dedication Event That Attendees Won't Forget

While a major building or renovation project can be grueling, everyone agrees it is something to celebrate. By hosting a stand-out dedication event, you not only show off all of your hard work, but also make a positive impression that will benefit your organization in countless ways.

So where do you begin planning a memorable dedication event?

First, come up with a wow factor, says Andrea Wyn Schall of A Wynning Event (Beverly Hills, CA), one of Southern California's premiere event planners and author of "Budget Bash — Simply Fabulous Events on a Budget." Whether it is through a unique invitation, a special feature at the event or the entertainment, your event must leave people feeling like they have experienced something special.

In addition to working behind the scenes at the Screen Actors Guild (SAG) awards, Wyn Schall's event planning business has helped numerous nonprofit agencies through the years. Her best advice for dedication events? Come up with a theme and roll with it for everything from the invitation to the party favors.

One popular theme for evening dedication events, she says, is to "go Hollywood" with lounge-style seating to make people feel like they are in an upscale club.

Another feature that drew oohs and aahs from attendees at a recent event was a large ice luge used to dispense drinks. A fusion of ice sculpture and drink dispenser, the large-scale ice block contained a banked ramp with two channels set in it. A drink, typically alcoholic, was poured from the top of the channel, chilling as it made its way to a glass at the bottom. To add even more punch, Wyn Schall says, they renamed the martinis that came out of the luge after some of the organization's high-profile board members and donors.

For more family-friendly events, Wyn Schall suggests coming up with a feature or entertainment that reflects the mission of the nonprofit. For example, have an artist create a mural that represents the organization in the facility. During the dedication, have the artist on hand to discuss the art piece with attendees as well as media.

You can get more mileage out of the mural concept by creating postcards, posters and stationery featuring the art piece to give as commemorative gifts or offer for purchase.

And when it comes to entertainment, Wyn Schall says that it is not always in your best interest to spend money to bring in a big-name person. Instead, focus on something that is pertinent to your organization. For instance, if your non-profit works with kids, have them come in and perform a dance number or a song at the dedication.

*Source: Andrea Wyn Schall, Event Planner, A Wynning Event, Beverly Hills, CA.*
*Phone (310) 279-5114. E-mail: andrea@budgetbashbook.com*

**ADMIT ONE**

**Promotion Idea**

Get additional event sponsors to underwrite the cost of creative advertising you otherwise couldn't afford (e.g., sky writing ads, outdoor billboards, television ads, etc.).

## 39. Two Ideas to Help Sell Seats at Your Next Event

Looking for great ways to raise more funds by selling seats to your next event?

Organizers of the Lights of Autumn fundraiser to benefit the Hospice of Huntington (Huntington, WV) have the following two options to help upgrade their experience and increase the amount raised on ticket sales:

✓ Open seating tickets for the event, which is a 2 1/2-hour dinner cruise on the Ohio River, complete with three live bands for entertainment, cost $125. For just $25 more, guests can upgrade to reserved seating.

✓ Groups of 10 or more are automatically upgraded to reserved seating.

Both of these options give guests the incentive to spend a little bit more or sell a few more tickets, which help increase the funds raised and make the event a success.

*Source: Shelly Betz, Director of Development and Community Relations, Hospice of Huntington, Inc., Huntington, WV. Phone (800) 788-5480.*
*E-mail: sbetz@hospiceofhuntington.org*

---

**Promotion Idea**

Deliver flyers to local schools encouraging staff to send them home with students.

**ADMIT ONE**

---

## 40. Engage New Audience With Teaming Event

Carrie Cook Bray, financial adviser with Merrill Lynch Global Wealth Management (Centerville, OH), says she is always searching for other women who are promoting their businesses or nonprofits. "I introduce my folks to them; they introduce their folks to me. As women, we prefer to meet numerous people versus hard-sell to a few."

That preference for a team-building approach to networking is the premise behind monthly Women, Wine and Wealth events that Bray organizes with three goals in mind:

1. Giving women opportunities to network with each other.
2. Introducing women to a woman-owned or woman-run local business or nonprofit.
3. Giving women financial advice in a comfortable setting.

The evening events include an hour of networking followed by a 15-minute presentation from a woman business owner or nonprofit executive and a 15-minute presentation on financial advice by Bray, including time for questions.

The March 2011 event featured representatives from Goodwill Easter Seals Miami Valley (Dayton, OH) promoting its vision services and radio reading services programs. Development Project Manager Angie Hoschouer says, "We felt that we had engaged those who were in attendance and that was the ultimate goal — to educate a new audience to our programs and services and have them take away information they hadn't known."

There is no cost to attend the event and no fundraising at the event. Typically 20 to 25 women attend each month, invited primarily through e-mail and social media outlets.

*Source: Carrie Cook Bray, Financial Advisor, Merrill Lynch Global Wealth Management, Centerville, OH. Phone (937) 312-2702. E-mail: carrie_bray@ml.com*
*Angie Hoschouer, Development Project Manager, Goodwill Easter Seals Miami Valley, Dayton, OH. Phone (877) 363-3303. E-mail: a.hoschouer@gesmv.org*

## 41. Combine Different Elements To Broaden Your Event's Appeal

To open your sports-themed fundraiser to more participants, add multiple elements at various competition levels that appeal to a wide range of ages and skill levels.

This approach has worked well for more than 10 years for the CVS/pharmacy Strong Legs Run to benefit Children's Healthcare of Atlanta (CHOA) of Atlanta, GA.

In addition to the event's main attractions — a 10K run and 5K walk/run — the race event features six elements from which the public can choose to support CHOA.

Renee Fraley, event coordinator, estimates an eighth of this year's $155,000 in proceeds came from these six other features, with 3,500 people participating in the main race and 1,200 in its other features.

Fraley outlines the six features offered in addition to the 10K run and 5K walk/run:

1. **2K Family Fun Walk or Run:** For $20 per adult and $15 per child (12 and under), a family can enter this two-mile walk or run in support of CHOA.

2. **Mascot Trot:** Children 12 and under race with mascots from their favorite Atlanta-area sports teams in front of Turner Field. Entrance fee: $12.

3. **CVS/pharmacy All Kids Can Race:** A 75-yard event for children age 12 and younger who have physical and developmental disabilities. Entrance fee: $12.

4. **Phantom Racer:** For individuals who wish to support CHOA but are unable to be present at the race. Entrance fee: $25.

5. **VIP Runner:** Participants who upgrade to VIP level receive access to a VIP area, post-race brunch, private restrooms and more. Entrance fee: $50.

6. **Team Participation:** Special division for corporate, community and school groups wishing to race as a team. Fee: $20 per team member.

*Source: Renee Fraley, Event Coordinator, Children's Healthcare of Atlanta, Atlanta, GA. Phone (404) 785-7315. E-mail: renee.fraley@choa.org*

### Promotion Idea

Collect testimonials from people who attended and loved last year's event. Then use those in promotional materials.

### Incentives Boost Event's Bottom Line

Looking for extra incentive to get your run/walk race participants involved in raising additional funds for your cause? Offer gift cards to popular area restaurants, shopping centers or entertainment venues.

Not only do gift cards add an element of excitement for race participants, gift card incentives can also boost your event's net proceeds.

This incentive works well for Children's Healthcare of Atlanta's CVS/pharmacy Strong Legs Run (Atlanta, GA), as participants are invited to connect with friends and family to collect pledges in support of their participation in the race. Depending on pledges raised, participants can earn gift certificates to a local mall or department store.

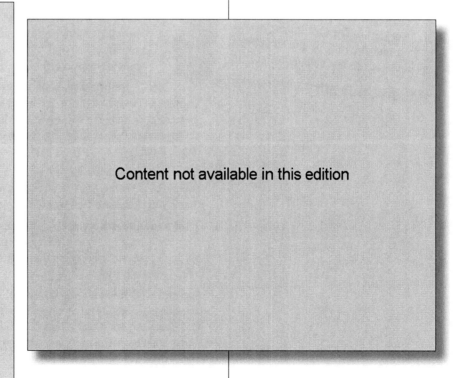

Content not available in this edition

## 42. Offer Event Choices to Boost Revenue, Attendance

Angie Hoschouer, development project manager, Goodwill Easter Seals Miami Valley (Dayton, OH) says offering prospective attendees a choice for their third annual fundraising event paid some worthwhile returns, increasing overall attendance by about 100 and boosting revenue by nearly $5,000 over the previous year.

To encourage more attendees, Hoschouer says they held both a breakfast and a lunch, whereas in the past they held just a breakfast.

Both events were one-hour affairs, featuring a video of three participants who told their stories. A participant's son also spoke at both events, telling how Easter Seals Adult Day Services helped him to take care of his aging mother during the day while he worked, and how she has received love and care while a participant in the program.

*Source: Angie Hoschouer, Development Project Manager, Goodwill Easter Seals Miami Valley, Dayton, OH. Phone (937) 528-6564.*
*E-mail: A.Hoschouer@gesmv.org. Website: www.gesmv.org*

### Increase Event Attendance

Want more people to attend your events? Make children a part of your program. Parents never miss an opportunity to see their little ones in the limelight. If you involve children in some capacity, their parents are bound to attend your event.

## 43. Keep Your Event Vibrant, Attract New Guests

It's not that you aren't grateful for the loyal supporters who always attend your special events, but attracting new people to your activities is the best way to continue to keep them vibrant. Here are some ideas to help you draw first-time visitors.

✓ **Build a theme around teams.** Best Friends or Co-workers are theme ideas that encourage existing supporters to bring a colleague or close friend to your event with them.

✓ **Keep up with chamber of commerce lists.** Look for newly established businesses in your community. Put them on your invitation list, and follow up with a phone call to the new entrepreneur to offer special pricing for all employees.

✓ **Build a Facebook event page.** Ask existing supporters with Facebook accounts to "like" your page, which shows their friends what is important to them. Include an RSVP link where their friends can see who else plans to attend. They may see that lots of their friends are going and decide to check it out.

✓ **Offer two-for-one event prices.** Your loyal supporters will be able to bring a friend for the same price as attending as a single — and you'll have a way to thank your longtime fans by allowing them to treat a friend to a fun venue.

✓ **Find a unique new venue.** If your family festival has always been held at City Park, look for an interesting alternative, like your local zoo, a botanical garden or art museum where there are new attractions and displays that people want to see anyway.

✓ **Feature well-known entertainment.** A favorite stand-up comic, acrobatic act, dance troupe, band or singer may be one of the easiest ways to bring new audiences to your event. Their fans may welcome the chance to attend the performance while supporting a worthy cause that is new to them.

### Promotion Idea

Use a marquee placed at a high-traffic location to get the message to the public. The cost is inexpensive, and you may be able to get it underwritten by a donor or business.

### ADMIT ONE

## 44. Mix Fun, Learning

A great recipe for success offers family events in which parents can see their children have fun while actually learning something. Want an even better recipe? Provide activities for children and parents to do together.

A museum treasure hunt, a hands-on heirloom craft or art project or the chance to work side by side planting or harvesting a vegetable garden for the community food shelter are guaranteed ways to bring families to your special event.

**ADMIT ONE**

### Promotion Idea

Pitch periodic feature stories leading up to your event — features about the event's unique venue, how funds being raised will be used, a look back at past events and more.

## 45. Girls Nite Out: Drawing Women to Your Event

Since its inception in 2007, the Girls Nite Out event (Northfield, MN) has drawn nearly 500 women for an evening of shopping, sales and female bonding, all for a good cause. More than 50 local businesses stay open late on a Saturday to offer special discounts on merchandise and services as part of the downtown shopping and social event.

The evening of the event, attendees gather at Northfield's Bridge Square to buy $10 wristbands that gain them admission to the specialty shops lining Division Street, plus special perks of the night including facials, makeovers, Tarot readings, appetizers, in-store drawings and manicures as well as special discounts from 5 to 9 p.m.

After the shopping draws to a close, participants go to the Grand Event Center to be entertained with live music, dancing, desserts and are eligible to win the grand prize of a $1,000 shopping spree in downtown Northfield, plus more prizes.

"When we started this event, we just wanted to have a great night for women where they could let loose and have a night off," says Ally Beyer, event cochair. "It has become a yearly highly anticipated tradition for many groups of friends. It is the most amazing feeling to be at The Grand and to look around at the ages ranging from 21 to 80, everyone having a blast. It truly is a remarkable event and a wonderful way to say thank you to the women of Northfield."

Not only do local businesses benefit from the event, a local charitable cause receives a portion of the proceeds from ticket sales each year. The recipient for the most recent event was the nonprofit Women in Northfield Giving Support (WINGS).

The event-planning committee works for months orchestrating the event, says Beyer, who shares innovative tips for drawing more women to your next event:

- **Advertise with flair.** Advertise in surrounding area newspapers with eye-catching colors and details about the event. The Girls Nite Out committee worked with a local artist to design a female-friendly invitation that became the impetus for the group's posters and advertisements.
- **Give attendees something new each year.** Add one new exciting thing to draw people in from the previous year, such as a $1,000 shopping spree grand prize. Heavily publicize the newly added item in ads, posters and on the invitations.
- **Posters, posters, posters.** Put up posters in local businesses at least six weeks before your event to get people excited!
- **Build support, excitement from the inside out.** Be sure to have a solid committee with go-getters. Delegate tasks and work together as a team. That, Beyer says, is what made Girls Nite Out Northfield such a huge success.

*Source: Ally Beyer, Cochair, Girls Nite Out, Northfield, MN.*

### Get the Community Talking

Ever notice that the most well-attended popular events are also the ones that people are talking about weeks ahead of time?
Get the word out. If you can get the public talking about your event in advance, it's well on its way to becoming a big hit.

## 46. Let Guests Be Part of a First

Is your community anticipating the opening of a new restaurant or gift shop or a fantastic season of the symphony or theatre?

Give guests an exclusive sneak peek. For that gourmet ice cream parlor opening soon, truck in samples to offer as desserts or in a sampling buffet. For that boutique with a ribbon cutting in the near future, invite the owner to set up a decorative display, create centerpieces for tables and provide gift certificates. Provide an exclusive preview of the upcoming theatre or symphony season with performance vignettes.

## 47. Major Raffle Item, Early Ticket Sales Boost Event Success

The Whitney Zoo-To-Do Gala is the pinnacle annual event for the Audubon Nature Institute (New Orleans, LA) — a partnership of 10 museums and parks. The gala draws nearly 3,800 attendees a year. Zoo-To-Do and Kids Zoo-To-Do annual events such as the gala raise more than $1 million annually to help underwrite creation and/or restoration of Audubon Zoo exhibits.

Ann Heslin, director of Zoo-To-Do events for the Audubon Nature Institute, shares tips for presenting a gala that keeps members coming back year after year:

❑ **Offer earlybird event ticket discounts.** Earlybird ticket sales, which give members a 20-percent discount on gala tickets if purchased by a specific date, are promoted primarily through a Web-based campaign.

❑ **Offer a luxury raffle item.** The Zoo-To-Do office and gala chairman solicit a local car dealer to donate a new vehicle to be raffled to the public. Tickets are $100 each and are limited to 1,000 chances. Raffle tickets are sold through direct mail, online and by distributing flyers to area retailers.

❑ **Offer electronic event ticketing.** Electronic tickets offer greater flexibility to guests since they can be printed directly from a website. Zoo-To-Do Gala, Kids Zoo-To-Do and raffle tickets are sold through OMNI Ticketing System (www.omniticket.com). Heslin recommends that any nonprofit organization do cost and service comparisons before proceeding with a ticketing system.

❑ **Offer an alternative event that includes members' children.** Kids Zoo-To-Do at the Audubon Nature Institute offers an alternative event geared for children on an alternate date from the annual gala. This event is the zoo's premiere event for children, offering live entertainment, play land, dancing and more. Tickets are $25 for members, $35 for nonmembers, offering a more casual event for families and creating an additional revenue source for the institute.

*Source: Ann Heslin, Director of Zoo-To-Do Events, Audubon Nature Institute, New Orleans, LA. Phone (504) 212-5459. E-mail: aheslin@AudubonInstitute.org. Website: www.AudubonInstitute.org*

### Promotion Idea

Commission an artist or photographer to create a limited edition item that can be given to event attendees who purchase advance tickets by a certain deadline.

ADMIT ONE

# 48. Offer a Sneak Preview of Entertainment

Whether it's through a TV, radio or newspaper interview or by placing performers at street corners or in the mall, get your entertainment's name and genre out. This is especially important if you're bringing in someone with an unusual presentation or unknown name.

Give your community a preview of what to expect and you'll both:

1. Spike interest in your cause, and

2. Help possible attendees overcome their hesitation to attend because the event, sight-unseen, seems too far out of their comfort zone.

**ADMIT ONE**

### Promotion Idea

Create a special section on your website that focuses on promoting your special event and allows visitors to register or purchase tickets online.

# 49. Custom Facebook Page Boosts Event Attendance

Imagine if you could triple attendance at one of your organization's long-standing events. Technology and social media can help make that happen, says Michael Howard, principal, At Your Service Business Consulting (Albany, NY).

Howard says he helped the local chapter of the Leukemia and Lymphoma Society (LLS) use the social networking site Facebook to increase attendance at its annual Taste of Compassion wine tasting event from an average of 250 attendees to nearly 650 over two years.

To do so, Howard designed an expanded mini-website page, known as a custom Facebook page, which allowed more photos and copy, PDF downloads and links to buy tickets. The Taste of Compassion Facebook page brought people involved with other parts of the organization in as fans. That included some 1,200 persons involved in the Team in Training marathon fundraising program, where athletes run half and full marathons to raise money. Howard says Facebook opened up a huge communications medium with those people — most of whom are younger — about how cool the wine tasting event is.

Regular updates on prizes, wineries and ticket sales had a viral effect, leading sponsors and friends of sponsors to become fans.

He says the first year using Facebook, they saw attendance grow from 250 to 400, which also led to a change in venue. The following year, the event drew 650.

Howard says Facebook also serves as a cross-promotion platform for all of the organization's events throughout the year.

"Fans rarely leave, so it is easy to place a post on the Taste of Compassion page for their spring event, which also has its own Facebook page," he says. "The LLS chapter has its own page for communication, not related to a particular event. All of the organization's pages keep them in communication with their most likely supporters, creating a community around supporters of the organization and allowing them to communicate with each other. This can't be achieved with traditional fundraising mailings and telemarketing campaigns."

*Source: Michael Howard, Principal, At Your Service Business Consulting, Albany, NY. Phone (518) 449-2420. E-mail: mhoward@consider-done.com. Website: www.consider-done.com*

### Consider Utility Bills: A Hidden Publicity Tool

Looking for a creative way to publicize your upcoming special event? Why not include an eye-catching insert in your city's utility bills?

Not only is this a cost-effective technique to promote your message throughout the year, it also serves as a means to garner attention for your special event. And including an invitation or awareness-raising piece in this format will mean your information will get to most of the households in your community.

Think of all the potential constituents you may be reaching who are not familiar with your cause or who may not know how to get involved.

## 50. Give Special Access

Let folks know your event will give them an insider's look at an area that is normally off limits, such as:

- A tour of a church belfry or community clock tower, with maintenance persons on hand to field questions.
- A behind-closed-doors tour of a museum or art center, with curators stationed in various locations, unpacking a new exhibit or preparing for a display.
- Admittance to a press room during a benefit ballgame or TV control room during a telethon.
- First entry into a new facility before a public ribbon cutting.
- The chance to be the first to hit the lanes at a new bowling alley.
- An after-hours tour of your medical facility's operating room or other non-public area.

## 51. It's Never Too Early to Send Save-the-date Cards

Save-the-date announcements are a surefire way to create enthusiasm about upcoming events and programs long before you finalize all event details.

"We have used save-the-dates in our newsletters, press releases and even on our website," says Kristin Van Nort, communications coordinator, The Oklahoma United Methodist Foundation (Oklahoma City, OK). "I think it is important to give our readers and supporters some anticipation about what is ahead and what they can look forward to.

"With an important upcoming event or program, we want to make sure everyone knows it is coming and has it on their calendar. It also keeps us accountable to a deadline to follow through with the upcoming information in a timely manner."

They send save-the-date cards or post save-the-date announcements online up to five months before a planned event.

"Having program or event changes is a risk you take with using save-the-dates, but I think the reward of attendance and participation is much greater than the risk," says Van Nort. "We have had to reissue a save-the-date card after a luncheon date had to be changed. We immediately sent out new cards."

They also use the announcements to encourage participation, she says: "During visits with donors and supporters, we will get questions about the teased event or program. I definitely believe save-the-date notifications enhance our event attendance. Attendance is typically down for those that we do not send out cards or post information on our website or in our newsletter."

For organizations considering whether to use this communications tool, Van Nort offers this advice: "Organizations should carefully choose which events and programs warrant a save-the-date notification. Overusing this type of announcement/promotion may take away from its success."

If your organization does not have the budget to mail save-the-date cards, borrow the foundation's method of posting save-the-date announcements online, in your publications and in your press materials.

*Source: Kristin Van Nort, Communications Coordinator, The Oklahoma United Methodist Foundation, Oklahoma City, OK. Phone (800) 259-6863. E-mail: kvannort@okumf.org*

### Promotion Idea

Two to three months prior to an event purchase a bus ad. Officials at a north-eastern college used this technique and said it was a hit and an inexpensive promotion method.

ADMIT ONE

## 52. Cookie Walk Event Draws Large Crowd, Interest

Seven years hosting an event allows for refinement and growth.

The West Des Moines Christian Church (West Des Moines, IA) annually hosts the Great Cookie Walk, drawing more than 500 guests each year to purchase specialty and gourmet cookies prepared by church members. Proceeds of $8,000 earned from the cookie sales and silent auction at the 2010 event went to the Youth Justice Initiative (Des Moines, IA), an organization geared to integrating young offenders back into the community.

To draw this type of large crowd and interest, event organizers have made their cookie walk stand out from others in their area in the following ways:

❑ Tables are decorated and adorned with formal linens.

❑ Most of the cookies are specialty and gourmet offerings including intricately decorated sugar cookies, shortbreads and bars. Crowd favorites include peanut butter mouse cookies with licorice tails and a six-layer chocolate mint bar cookie.

❑ Organizers ensure bakers create unique offerings to draw guests. At this event, one station offered extra-large gingerbread cookies that could be personalized.

❑ Offering advance orders. Organizers of the Great Cookie Walk allowed guests to pre-order to ensure additional sales.

❑ All table attendees wear aprons decorated with a cookie motif and male attendees wear chef hats. Volunteers selling cookies wear gloves to keep the event sanitary.

❑ Volunteers are asked to commit to a specific number of cookies they'll contribute to the sale. Event planners organize baking days in a commercial kitchen to create an assembly line of bakers who crank out hundreds of dozens of cookies.

❑ Cookies are priced by the pound. Cashier tables feature scales for easy weighing and pricing.

❑ Organizers set up multiple cashier tables. The idea behind any cookie walk is that customers can easily move around the table to purchase multiple cookies. Make sure your event space flows and that you offer multiple locations to check out.

❑ Keep guests entertained by offering additional activities such as music, silent auctions and/or drawings. The Great Cookie Walk held a drawing every 30 minutes offering guests cookie-related prizes such as cookie-mix-in-a-jar blends.

*Source: Karen Townsend, Great Cookie Walk Coordinator, West Des Moines Christian Church, West Des Moines, IA. Phone (515) 223-1876. Website: www.wdmcc.org*

**ADMIT ONE**

### Promotion Idea

If your event includes food, come up with a clever food theme to help attract publicity.

### Add a Contest to Excite and Engage Volunteer Bakers, Chefs

Hosting a bake sale or other food-oriented fundraiser? Create a food-based side contest to generate more interest in your event.

At the Great Cookie Walk put on by the West Des Moines Christian Church (West Des Moines, IA), baking volunteers enjoy the heat of competition through a planned contest. Use rules and guidelines offered for the Great Cookie Walk as a starting point to create your contest:

• Contestants must be signed up to bake cookies by stated deadline.

• Submit your name, phone number, e-mail address and contest recipe as stated in the official rules.

• Bakers for selected recipes will be notified by designated date that their entry has been accepted.

• Bring dough and all decorations to bake one dozen cookies at the designated commercial kitchen. Time slots in 90- to 120-minute increments will be available between the designated hours.

• Cookies will be judged by qualified bakers on taste, presentation and festive appearance.

• Bakers preparing the first place and two runner-ups' cookies will bring 10 dozen of their special cookies on sale day.

• Selections will be uniquely identified, promoted and displayed on the front entry table the day of the sale. Prizes will also be awarded to the top three cookie bakers chosen for 2011.

## 53. Use Simple, Effective Ways to Improve E-invites

Electronic invitations allow you to adhere to your planning budget and still send an impactful, meaningful message. Use these tips to create effective, eye-catching e-invites:

✓ Write a subject line with a sense of urgency offering a deadline or date by which you need action.

✓ Provide all event details in the e-mail. The basics such as where, when, why, how and what time should be included.

✓ Personalize your invitation. For example, using the send personally option in Microsoft Outlook allows you to e-mail an invitation to multiple recipients in a format that will appear as if it was sent individually to each.

✓ Add your company logo to your e-invite and use graphics to give your electronic invitation the wow factor.

✓ Build your e-mail invite so it can display on mobile phone applications.

✓ E-mail a follow-up invite to get more attention and incite nonresponders to act.

### Build Your Invitation List

It's sometimes easy to overlook the obvious. To maximize attendance for your next event, be sure to invite:

1. Everyone on your mailing list.
2. Those who attended past events.
3. Residents in particular ZIP codes.
4. Chamber of commerce members.
5. Elected officials.
6. Persons known for attending other nonprofits' events.
7. Members of the media.
8. Those who have used your nonprofits' services.
9. All current and past board members and volunteers.

## 54. Winning Invitation Tips

One of the most important tasks when planning a major event such as an open house for your new facility is designing invitations that will get the people to the major event.

Andrea Wyn Schall, professional event planner with A Wynning Event (Beverly Hills, CA), shares three tips to make your invitation stand out and create a healthy buzz about your event:

1. **List board members or high-profile people associated with the fundraiser or dedication event on the invitation.** Even if someone is unfamiliar with your organization, they may be personal or business associates of those people and will show up at your event to support them.

2. **Don't ignore the power of e-mail and social media to spread the word about your event.** Create an e-invite and have your board members e-mail them out to everyone in their address books. Or have them post the e-invite on their social media profile. Wyn Schall says that if each of your 10 board members has 100 friends, you've opened yourself up to 1000 more people potentially.

3. **Get creative!** Is there a unique way you can deliver the invites? Some special way you can package them? The invitation is the first impression of the event, and you want it to stand out.

*Source: Andrea Wyn Schall, Event Planner, A Wynning Event, Beverly Hills, CA. Phone (310) 279-5114. E-mail: andrea@budgetbashbook.com*

### Promotion Idea

Send an early invitation to last year's attendees, offering them a free premium if they register early for this year's event.

ADMIT ONE

## 55. Book a Pseudo-celebrity

Wonder Woman, Superman or Merlin the Magician may be fictional characters, but why not make them real for your special event? Tap your local college or community theatre for persons who can dress the part of a fantasy person in literature, comic books or the silver screen and mingle with the crowd.

Choose names to play up your theme. For example, bring "Gilligan's Island"-theme characters to your beach party, and invite your guests along for a three-hour tour.

### Offer Motivating Incentives

Consider offering incentives for achieving certain goals or completing specific tasks. For example, a Chicago nonprofit that hosted a celebrity author as its event speaker provided a personalized, autographed book to any volunteer who sold 15 or more tickets to the event —a simple incentive that helped generate record attendance.

## 56. Offer Entertaining Promotions

Hurry up and wait is an all too familiar phrase to many people, especially when stuck in traffic, waiting for an appointment at the doctor's office or sitting in the drive-through line for a sandwich at lunch. When the time comes to promote your next special event, think of ways to entertain people who may have a few minutes to think of nothing more important than your announcement.

- **Dress for success with costumes.** Ask volunteers in theme clothing to walk through your local mall or city park with save-the-date signs, greeting morning or evening joggers, parents and children. Team up volunteers who can sing or dance for impromptu performances. Seek advance permission when needed — mall staff or business owners may alert media and draw coverage. Have an instant camera ready to pose for a free picture with people you meet, and place a sticker with event time and date on it.

- **Team with local fast food franchises.** Look for independently owned stores whose owners may be willing to put a poster in their drive-through lines or flyers with a free drink coupon with event details in take-out bags.

- **Find a busy but safe intersection.** Slow-moving rush hour traffic is a good place to reach commuters. Work with a business owner or city officials to allow groups of your volunteers wearing bright T-shirts or holding banners to draw attention to your event, waving and smiling at passing cars. Ask morning radio hosts to mention them and your event during traffic reports.

- **Create a brief trivia quiz and contest about your organization and event.** Ask local medical clinics, banks or other locations with lobbies and waiting room tables to set out a small stack along with a drop box for completed quizzes. Each entrant can provide a contact e-mail or street address so you can send correct answers with an incentive to attend (e.g., free ticket or T-shirt). You also will have their contact information for future events.

### ADMIT ONE

### Promotion Idea

If appropriate, encourage civic organizations and faith-based organizations to publicize your event to their members.

## 57. Create a Plan to Beat Last Year's Attendance

If you repeat a particular fundraising event each year, how much time do you put into setting attendance goals designed to surpass the previous years' numbers? That key aspect of your event deserves a written plan.

Some of the components of that plan may include:

**Making every effort to get previous guests to attend —**

- Offer special perks to anyone who attended last year's event — special seating or parking or an opportunity to attend a preview of the event.

- Get last year's attendees signed up before anyone else (e.g., early bird invitation).

**Pursuing specific strategies aimed at attracting new attendees —**

- Get previous years' attendees involved in inviting friends and associates to this year's event.

- Add new features to your event that may attract those who had no previous interest (e.g., special entertainment, a celebrity, a one-of-a-kind auction item).

Set an attendance goal for your next event and back up the increase with specific strategies aimed at meeting that goal.

## 58. Involve More Guests With Entertaining Activities

Raising funds for and increasing awareness of your mission may be the purpose of your event, but many who attend will see it as an opportunity to have fun and socialize.

Here are some tips you can use to help increase audience involvement and entertainment.

- **Create a central attraction in the middle of the room**, like a large cupcake display or dance floor, so everyone feels involved regardless of seating assignment.

- **Brief your entertainment on the people in the audience**, including amusing stories the entertainers can bring up in their routines.

- **Adapt an audience participation game** like "Let's Make a Deal" or "The Price Is Right" to your program where any guest has a chance to be on stage or win a prize.

- **Offer a scavenger hunt.** Compile a list of common items (shoelace, nail clipper, pocketknife, flashlight) that guests might not normally carry to a party. Ask those who have the item to share why they brought them.

- **Try "Name That Tune!"** Everyone has a party horn. Play snippets of music to see who can identify it first by blowing their horn. Let the top players compete for a grand prize.

- **Feature some popular casino games.** Have a few that require skill, like blackjack, and others like roulette or dice that anyone can play.

- **Hire a cartoonist.** A quick sketch artist can float between tables drawing guests, and then make a display at the end of the evening for all to view.

- **Suggest a table switch.** Put five or six different colors of decoration on individual desserts. Ask each person to have the last course with someone else who has a green flower, an orange star or a purple crown.

---

**Promotion Idea**

Hire an impersonator to come to your community and do a live radio interview and community appearance to draw attention to your event.

ADMIT ONE

---

**Book a Celebrity**

Give guests the chance to mingle with someone famous — a local celebrity, such as your symphony's new conductor; a widely known and respected former resident; or even a person whose claim to fame is being part of a reality TV show.

---

## 59. Sell Themed Keepsakes to Bring Back Attendees Year After Year

Whether offered to help promote your event in advance, used as admittance tickets or simply sold or given away to draw attendees, items commemorating your special event can help draw a crowd.

Here are just a few such items to consider offering as mementos or keepsakes to make people come back year after year to add to their collection:

✓ Artist-designed event posters, T-shirts, plates, mugs or totes

✓ Commemorative lapel pins

✓ Silicone cause bracelets, magnetic car ribbons or car antenna decorations

✓ Silver charms or key chain fobs

✓ Wall or desk calendars

✓ Framed and dated photo from event

✓ Christmas or other holiday ornament

### Want to Attract Seniors?

When your event is geared to senior citizens, be sure to cater to their particular needs in the following ways:

• Make parking easily accessible to the event or offer valet parking.

• Consider having escorts available to usher them to their seats.

• Offer sufficient seating to avoid prolonged periods of standing.

• Provide an adequate sound system to ensure everyone can hear what's being said.

• Offer menu items that are compatible with seniors and will appeal to them.

## 60. Timing, Function Boost Ribbon-cutting Attendance

You have a new location, a new building or newly remodeled space. All are good reasons to invite the community to celebrate. Planning and practicality can help ensure good attendance at your event.

For your ribbon-cutting, be sure to:

❑ **Determine best time of day**. Tailor event hours to the audience you hope to attract. An early morning coffee with breakfast pastries or late morning ceremony with sandwiches for lunch can be convenient for business crowds. Make it convenient for them to attend before work or during the noon hour. Start on time and limit speeches, so busy professionals can return to work.

❑ **Ask your local chamber of commerce for ideas**. While you may be planning your organization's first and only ribbon-cutting ceremony, your chamber of commerce can be an experienced resource not only for helping you formulate your plans, but publicizing the event to other members and even helping you schedule local officials to speak.

❑ **Give plenty of notice to invitees and vendors**. A midweek luncheon or cocktail-hour ceremony may take some advance planning for professionals and executives. They will enjoy an opportunity to network and socialize, as long as they can get it into their calendars in time. Florists, caterers and photographers may need to know at least a month beforehand.

❑ **Target current and potential customers**. You want your event to showcase the facility and services in the most positive light to show current customers how they can expect even better results, and expose potential new customers to the advantages you offer. If they have families or young children, consider an open house with department tours, entertainment and refreshments after your ribbon cutting. A weekend party that lasts several hours encourages them to stay and get to know you, and allows more people to attend as schedules permit.

### ADMIT ONE

### Promotion Idea

Place large-scale presentation boards on easels in businesses' lobbies.

## 61. Tips to Elevate Attendance at Winter Receptions

Winter holidays bring a full schedule of receptions and parties for busy persons like your volunteers and supporters. Here are ideas for hosting a memorable, festive open house or reception, no matter the size of your guest list or budget:

1. **Choose a fun winter theme.** While Christmas or Hanukkah are logical choices, think also of snowmen, plaid fabrics, fragrant candles, evergreen sprigs with pine cones and cardinals, gingerbread houses or hearty gourmet foods with unique varieties of beer or wine. Each lends itself to a warm welcome.

2. **Offer sweet treats.** Use colorful seasonal candy liberally in decorating. Tie to place cards, napkins and wreaths, scatter on tables or have Santa hand it out. Offer vegetables and dip, cheeses and nuts for variety.

3. **Give a photo souvenir.** Stock up on Polaroid film (or digital film and a desktop printer) and pre-made cardboard seasonal photo frames. Encourage guests to have pictures taken with Santa, Rudolph, a snowman display or a gallery of life-sized cutouts of popular characters.

4. **Choose a festive location.** Check availability of a Victorian bed-and-breakfast with large reception area, museum or art gallery, or party room of a popular restaurant. They may already be decorated for the holidays, allowing you to concentrate on added attractions like strolling carolers, magicians or a string quartet.

5. **Balloons, lights and music.** Nothing says party like balloon archways and centerpieces tied with shiny, long strings (so guests can see each other across the table). Add twinkling lights and taped music like jazz renditions of holiday tunes.

6. **Be flexible about time of day.** Busy supporters may thoroughly enjoy an early holiday breakfast buffet. Crepes, pancakes, waffles, fruits, meats and fresh juices offer limitless menu options. An afternoon tea might include dainty sandwiches or cookies, scones, pastries and even a flute of champagne (tie curly ribbon on the stems).

7. **Personalize gifts for each guest.** Give an ornament or ceramic mug, and have the best calligraphers in your ranks ready with paint pens to decorate them.

8. **Festive face painting.** Children can ask for Rudolph's red nose, an elf's sparkling eyes or other holiday-theme characters with colorful makeup and glitter.

9. **Admission: can of food.** Host a party where admission is a non-perishable canned item or pair of mittens. Serve flavored popcorn, hot cider, cocoa, coffee and donated baked goods. Choose a location near shopping areas, giving shoppers a chance to relax and re-energize while listening to vocal groups or holiday music.

10. **Holiday costumes and characters.** Let the performers among your volunteers use costumes in your organization's name in public places. Victorian-costumed carolers strolling through a mall or a happy Ebenezer Scrooge tossing wrapped candies to the kids spreads good cheer and offers positive media photo opportunities.

---

### Promotion Idea

Promote your event via the Internet through e-mails, bulletin boards, listservs, blogs and more.

ADMIT ONE

---

### Ways to Weave in Winter Wonder

Winter can be a magical time. Here are three ideas to capture that magic for your guests:

✓ **Boxes, ribbons and bows galore!** Go all out decorating with gift boxes of all sizes. Artistically wrap packages, from refrigerator- to diamond ring-sized, to use as archways, centerpieces, and open containers of popcorn and candy.

✓ **Coffee, anyone?** Nothing goes better on a cold winter night than a hot steaming mug of indulgence. Create a specialty coffee/cappuccino/cocoa bar and watch guests gather. Scatter plenty of small tables with comfortable chairs throughout the room, nestling some away in areas decorated with holiday lights. Have a cookie decorating area for guests to frost a gingerbread man to eat or take home.

✓ **Pull out the Santa ties.** Encourage festive but comfortable attire. Instead of business casual or cocktail attire try favorite holiday outfit.

---

## 62. Give 'Em Something Free

Want more people at your golf tourney? Bring in a golf pro to offer free putting tips. Need more bodies at your free outdoor concert? Provide free shuttle service from a centrally located parking venue. Have plenty of persons coming to one event but need to boost attendance at a second? Offer persons with tickets to the first event two-for-one tickets to the second.

## 63. Boost Your Event's Ability To Attract Young Donors

Today's young professionals may very well be tomorrow's major givers, if they aren't already there. Attracting these fresh faces to your special events — and, ultimately, to your donor pool — requires going beyond the same old stale rules.

If you're hoping to reach a younger market with your events, the following tips can help you get started:

- ❑ **Reach them where they live.** Everything today is about social media and digital technology. Make sure someone on your staff understands and is comfortable using sites like MySpace (www.myspace.com), Facebook (www.facebook.com) and Twitter (www.twitter.com) to generate excitement and share updates about the event. Consider having an event volunteer blog about the planning process. Post testimonials on YouTube (www.youtube.com) from people your organization helps.

- ❑ **Plan for the future.** Capture e-mail addresses of attendees, clarifying how you intend to use this information. Then follow through and keep these new donors in the loop, using e-mail alerts to let them know what's going on at your organization.

- ❑ **Think green.** Many young people are eco-minded and may respond more favorably to e-mailed save-the-date cards and invitations than traditional paper invitations. This saves your organization time and money too.

- ❑ **Consider holding an event just for them.** Many standard special events (e.g., galas, auctions, etc.) may not appeal to younger generations. Create an event that targets their interests and make sure it is planned by other young professionals, preferably some who are already strong supporters of your organization.

- ❑ **Make it exclusive.** Consider a sought-after venue with a hot food or drink trend (e.g., martini bar) and limit ticket numbers. Once you create a buzz with this premiere event, you can host future events at larger (but still trendy) venues.

### Offer Multiple Options At Event

Hope to attract large numbers of participants to your event? Be sure to include sufficient options that appeal to many people.

Exhibits, tours, differing forms of entertainment, opportunities to socialize, lectures and more all provide for multiple reasons to attend an event. Consider your target audience. If you're appealing to young families, for instance, consider child care and entertainment for youth.

A word of caution, however: If you promise something, deliver more than was expected. Doing so will help ensure large crowds for repeat events.

### Promotion Idea

Distribute free tickets to a deserving group of children or adults who might not otherwise be able to attend your event. Invite the press to be on hand as you distribute the tickets.

ADMIT ONE

## 64. Online Seating Chart Helps Sell Event Tickets

Here's a crowd-pleasing way to increase ticket sales for your next sit-down event: Put a seating chart on your website and let event attendees choose where they will sit.

Content not available in this edition

That's what officials with the Traverse City Area Chamber of Commerce (Traverse, MI) did for the first time last year, and every limited-seating event that used the chart in 2010 sold out, says Communications Coordinator Nate Jorgensen.

Jorgensen uses the software program Adobe Photoshop to create the chart (shown at left), creating different layers to represent the available and reserved seats. The website is updated daily.

"The chart shows how the event is filling up and encourages members and guests to buy their tickets," says Jorgensen.

Chamber staff use the same techniques to create a virtual version of the annual business expo.

*Source: Nate Jorgensen, Communications Coordinator, Traverse City Area Chamber of Commerce, Traverse City, MI. Phone (231) 947-5075. E-mail: jorgensen@tcchamber.org*

## 65. Promote Notable Guests

If a notable person within your community RSVPs to your annual event invitation, why not use that as leverage to entice other prominent guests?

Acquiring a Who's Who guest list can help draw larger attendance at your primary events. Try the following tips to creating a Who's Who event:

• Prior to sending out your mass invitation list, secure notables from your community to attend your event. Personally invite the mayor, area celebrities and prominent professionals to attend. When these notables agree to attend, ask to use their names to promote the event.

  • Create a Notable Guests or Who's Who section on your mass invitations, e-invites, website and publicity materials that offers a list of prominent guests and a brief quote from each individual about your organization and why they wish to attend.

  • Create color-coded nametags for notable guests to wear at the event so others may seek them out. Get their approval before doing so.

  • Ask a notable guest or two to speak on behalf of your organization the night of the event for an added special touch.

**Promotion Idea**

Utilize various community agencies to promote the event (e.g., recreation association, park district, sheriff's department, etc.).

ADMIT ONE

## 66. Steps Boost Ticket Sales

The financial success of a special event is often based on ticket sales. That's why it's so important that everyone involved takes responsibility for getting tickets sold. This is especially true if you are relying on volunteers for significant ticket sales.

To boost ticket sale success — and ultimately the success of your event overall:

- Plan backwards: The amount of revenue you want to generate will dictate both number of tickets you need to sell and ticket price. From there you can determine number of ticket sellers needed and minimum number of tickets each volunteer will need to sell.

- Get everyone involved in planning the event — not just those on the ticket committee — to agree to a minimum number of ticket sales.

- Agree that if volunteers cannot sell the agreed-to minimum ticket number, they will be responsible for buying the tickets they hold.

- Use the pyramid method of selling: A certain number of captains are responsible, in turn, for enlisting a minimum number of ticket sellers.

- Make it appealing for attendees to purchase a group of tickets (e.g., table of eight). Provide corresponding benefits for those who purchase a group/table of tickets — preferred seating, special favors, recognition, etc.

- Use friendly competition to encourage ticket sales. Offer an incentive, for instance, to any who sells a certain number of tickets by a particular date.

- For an annual event, allow veteran volunteers the privilege of selling tickets to those who have purchased from them in previous years.

- Provide event sponsors with a limited number of tickets for their employees as a perk.

> **Tips for Selling Tickets**
>
> Buy inexpensive buttons for volunteers, staff and others to wear, both on and off the job, that read: "Ask Me About Tickets to the XYZ Agency's Holiday Gala!" Keep the persons stocked in tickets to sell to impulse buyers, co-workers and other persons they encounter.

## 67. Three Ways to Maximize Major Event Publicity And Boost Attendance

Some special events impact your organization beyond a mere press release, and you hope to maximize the positive attention they bring. Develop a variety of ways to share the news with different audiences, but in different ways.

1. **Share client testimonials**. Your organization has been named top provider of services in your field by an independent group. Ask some of the most compelling clients you have served to go on camera or on the record for commercials, advertisements and feature stories that you can use throughout the year.

2. **Spotlight your benefactors**. A longtime supporter has left your institution a bequest that will allow you to build an addition, or ensures continuity of services for years to come. Who is or was this person? Write an article about his or her life, association with your organization and reasons for choosing you for this major gift. Explain how it will positively impact the community.

3. **Host a celebration activity**. Invite the community to share in your good fortune by holding an open house, family festival or free concert that trumpets your good news while also showing your gratitude. Publicity for the event should center on the reason for the celebration, and result in free media coverage.

> ADMIT ONE
>
> **Promotion Idea**
>
> Enlist a celebrity master of ceremonies whose reputation will help garner additional pre-event publicity.

## 68. Involve 50 Volunteers in Staging Your Next Open House

Calendars are checked and the caterer is saving the date. Your organization's open house is set. Almost. Before the big day, add this additional job to your to-do list: Recruit 50 volunteers who will work as guides, greeters, set-up-and-break-down crew or tour guides.

Why have 50 volunteers on hand? Three reasons: 1) To pull off a great event, you could probably use the help; 2) Getting a minimum of 50 volunteers involved helps ensure a respectable crowd size (especially if those 50 help convince others to attend); and 3) An open house for your organization provides multiple opportunities for volunteers to get involved and better own your organization and its programs.

Utilize some of these techniques to find and encourage willing volunteers, and to be sure they will arrive on time and ready to help:

- **Contact the 10 most likely recruits first.** You probably know at least that many volunteers who consistently attend and assist with all public events. Ask each one to recruit a friend or two, and your task is half-complete.

- **Call on volunteers who have been unable to do other jobs.** There may be many volunteers who haven't been able to take recent larger assignments, but still wish to help. Ask them if they can spare a couple hours to fill a shift at the open house.

- **Remind those who have signed up with a phone call, e-mail and a postcard.** Phone each person two weeks prior to the event to confirm the time and duty, and to have a replacement if a conflict occurs. Follow up a week later with a postcard that thanks them for agreeing to serve (noting the hours they are scheduled). Include any information about where volunteers should check in before going to work.

- **Circulate copies of the volunteer schedule at a general meeting before the event.** List the names, times and jobs for each confirmed person, then ask for help to fill any open spaces. Seeing names and duties on paper looks official and reminds volunteers that their involvement is necessary to ensure the event's success.

- **Make volunteers feel special for helping.** Tell the individuals you wish to recruit that you are calling the most cordial and outgoing volunteers first. Add that the organization seeks to make a positive impression on visitors seeing your facility for the first time, and that their pleasant attitude is exactly what is needed.

- **Offer each person a small gift.** Once they sign up to help, give them a useful token of appreciation a day or two before the event. For example, a colorful pin or ribbon will identify them as a member of the team, along with a certificate or a fresh lapel flower to wear to the event. This considerate gesture will help visitors find the volunteers, and remind volunteers that you are both expecting and counting on them.

---

### Invite the Entertainment's Friends and Family

Assuming everyone involved with your event will work equally hard to generate attendance can be a mistake. For example, don't assume students performing in your madrigal dinner will tell their parents about the event. Obtain a mailing list from the choir director and send information directly to their parents. Likewise, if you're featuring a local church choir, make sure news of your event is featured in the church bulletin. Also, consider spending a Sunday morning in the church narthex selling tickets.

---

### Promotion Idea

Create walking billboards. Give employees/volunteers T-shirts with the message you want to promote and encourage them to walk around your community handing out T-shirts to passersby. You have created a number of walking billboards promoting your upcoming event.

ADMIT ONE

---

## 69. Increase International Attendance At Your Annual Conference

Looking to grow your organization's membership? Consider making your annual meeting more friendly to overseas attendants.

Organizations need not have overseas members to promote their meeting as a global event, says Dave Fellers, founder of Dave Fellers Consulting, LLC (Prairie Village, KS). "Members always receive lower convention fees, so if you can interest foreign professionals in your meeting, you will naturally grow your membership."

Outreach can begin as simply as booking international presenters and speakers, says Fellers. Personal relationships are also key. "Whenever your president is traveling, he or she should be meeting foreign speakers and executives and telling them about your association and its meeting."

Invite presidents of all major international organizations in your industry to your conference, he says. "Comp their registration fees (you don't need to pay for their travel or lodging) and look for opportunities to put them on the program. A panel session discussing trends in their countries is often an effective approach."

He also suggests an invitation-only meal for foreign and domestic executive directors, with each given a few minutes to share news and challenges of his/her respective area.

Robust international marketing is appropriate, but, Fellers cautions, don't bypass foreign associations by approaching their members directly.

Finally, he says, make sure efforts to attract international attendees complement a comprehensive membership strategy. "What membership categories will you offer? What type of benefits will you offer? What kinds of marketing will you use? These are the kinds of questions that need to be addressed in your strategic plan."

*Source: Dave Fellers, Founder, Dave Fellers Consulting, LLC, Prairie Village, KS.*
*Phone (847) 254-2700.*
*E-mail: dave@fellerskc.com.*
*Website: www.fellerskc.com*

### Promotion Idea

Schedule appearances on area television and radio shows that include two or three individuals who have benefited from your services. Mention your event at that time.

ADMIT ONE

Content not available in this edition

## 70. Tapping Wine-tasting Trend Brings First-time Event Success

The right blend of music, food and wine proved an enticing recipe for success for the Rhythm and Vine Benefit for Boys and Girls Clubs of Greater San Diego (San Diego, CA).

The April 2010 fundraiser drew 1,498 attendees and netted $104,266.

"In the organization's eyes, this event was a success," says Special Events Coordinator Shannon Frick. "Not only did it attract a large number of attendees who had no previous involvement with our organization, but we also raised a significant amount of money to help fund high-quality programs for the local youth who attend our clubs."

Frick says the event replaced an annual dinner auction that had taken place for 50 years.

"Our organization was in need of an event that could attract a broader audience throughout the county and state, to include individuals who have yet to be involved with the Boys and Girls Clubs," she says. "Our senior management and board of directors realized the trend of wine events.... With the guidance of Fast Forward Ventures (an El Cajon, CA-based event management and production agency), as well as other Boys and Girls Clubs throughout the country who have hosted similar events, we formulated an event plan.

"This is the only event of its kind to unite music, food and wine in such a grandiose fashion to provide a one-of-a-kind, fun event, while also supporting a very worthy — and local — cause," Frick says. "It has already become the most-attended event for our organization and will continue to grow each year. It has also become the most heavily marketed event for our organization, which is a very useful tool in offering corporate partners/sponsors media exposure within their event sponsorship."

Frick says a majority of event revenue comes through sponsorships, with additional funds coming from ticket sales ($75 for general admission, $125 for VIP status and $40 for designated driver status, which includes food but no alcoholic beverages).

She cites other factors for the event's success:

- **Volunteers.** Nearly 120 people helped with the event, including set-up, exhibitor check-in, guest registration, and managing the silent auction and entertainment.

- **Venue.** The event took place at a popular shopping mall in Escondido, CA. Frick says mall officials donated use of the space, and event organizers transformed the parking lot into a "bright, welcoming area where guests could enjoy the various tastings and entertainment our event had to offer."

- **Exhibitors and contributors.** From an exhibitor standpoint, the event is a great marketing opportunity, Frick says. "Many wineries, breweries, restaurants, gourmet food purveyors, etc. choose to participate to help market their product/brand."

*Source: Shannon Frick, Special Events Coordinator, Boys and Girls Clubs of Greater San Diego, San Diego, CA, (858) 866-0591, ext. 203. Website: www.rhythmandvine.org*

### Tips to Build Attendance

There are any number of ways to optimize attendance for a special event. Here's one approach to consider:

- To reach out to the entire community or target certain neighborhoods, establish a promotions or marketing committee made up of one or more people representing various neighborhoods. Assign responsibility to each for getting the word out (or selling tickets) to all residents within their designated territories.

### Promotion Idea

Get local restaurants and bars to display table tents promoting your event.

ADMIT ONE

## 71. Website Offers Guidelines for Hosting Record-setting Event

Few events attract and entertain like a Guinness Book of World Records competition. Nearly 50,000 potential record breakers contact Guinness officials each year to ask where to begin, according to www.guinnessworldrecords.com. The website provides many resources, including a tutorial on how to fill out an application form.

Here is a rundown of considerations the organization offers:

❑ **Register on the website.** Get a user name. Describe your idea or concept. Read the guidelines for Guinness' criteria for what constitutes a first or record in various categories. This information should help you to determine if your idea is feasible.

❑ **Complete the application.** This process is free, but takes time for Guinness researchers to evaluate. Allow plenty of time. You must apply for your record before the event, as Guinness will not accept results after the fact. Results are processed in the London office. A second celebration may be in order when your record is verified and you receive your certificate of achievement.

❑ **Read all the FAQs.** This section has a wealth of information about records most frequently broken, who holds the most records and what types of activities have earned certificates. You may get a unique idea of your own by reviewing achievements of record holders.

❑ **Learn about Guinness' paid services.** You can hire GWR adjudicators to help you apply, find the right record fit for your organization and to attend your event to present your certificate on the spot. Fast track applications are available for $600 U. S. dollars. While basic service is free, larger events may benefit from additional paid support and licensing.

❑ **Enjoy browsing the website links.** Read about amazing feats like the heaviest person ever dangled from a swallowed sword, longest time a person has sat in a rattlesnake-filled bathtub and other courageous endeavors. The more you study what others have done, the greater the inspiration for your own potential record.

### Break a Record

Who wouldn't want to be part of the world's (or their city's) biggest ice cream sundae? Line dance? Paper airplane toss? One Midwestern hospital sends area elementary schools thousands of neon-colored invitations to a benefit hockey game. Printed on the back are instructions to bring the invitation to the game to fold into a paper airplane for the community's largest paper airplane toss between periods. Students whose planes land in face-off circles win donated prizes.

## 72. Set Measurable Objectives

As you plan events for an upcoming year, set quantifiable objectives that will allow you to measure achievements and surpass previous years' accomplishments. Here are some examples to get your wheels turning:

• To generate $X in special event net income throughout this fiscal year.

• To attract X event attendees throughout the upcoming fiscal year.

• To plan and coordinate X events that attract the following targeted audiences (e.g., senior citizens, females, the wealthy).

• To increase first-time event attendees by no less than X percent in the upcoming fiscal year.

• To generate a minimum of $X in sponsorship revenue this fiscal year.

### Promotion Idea

Conduct a pre-event drawing that brings attention to your event and helps build excitement.

ADMIT ONE

## 73. Twitter-driven Event Draws Crowd in 15 Days

Pulling off the first-ever HoHoTO (Toronto, Canada) event — a party at Toronto's Mod Club in support of the community's food bank — was no small feat.

In just 15 days, the Toronto technology community generated enough interest for the event to raise $25,000 for the Daily Bread Food Bank, solely by using their connections and marketing the event via Twitter (www.twitter.com). The event is pronounced hoe-hoe-TEE-oh, in recognition of the holiday season and Toronto's nickname, T.O.

Co-organizer Michael O'Connor Clarke offers tips for making a Twitter-generated event more of a success:

### A single tweet probably won't do it.

"That's not how Twitter works. For ideas to take off on Twitter, you need a network effect to happen — the idea has to spread organically, picking up traction and repetitions along the way. For this, either the idea must be highly compelling and impactful, or you need a lot of people to get behind the idea. You need to be able to reach a broad network of interested people who will spread the news for you."

### You can't create network effects overnight.

"No organization should expect to be able to jump into Twitter (or other social media channels such as blogging, Facebook, YouTube, etc.) and immediately see benefits. It takes time to build a community of followers, friends and interested parties who will help you to get the word out when you have something to say. Start now — if you're not already active on Twitter, you should be. You need to become immersed in the community you're going to want to influence; it's the only way to really understand it. If you don't get it (and a lot of people just don't — that's OK), then hire someone who does."

### Spend a lot of time listening.

"Before you engage with a Twitter audience, you need to understand who they are, what they're talking about, what they're interested in, who they follow, what motivates them, what they dislike. There are lots of monitoring services and search engines you can use to do your research before you dive in. Radian6 (www.radian6.com) is a great software tool for this kind of preparatory work. The thing is: Social media is about conversation. These conversations are multi-faceted, bidirectional and already happening. If you just jump into a conversation that's already going on without spending the time to listen to what's being said, you're only going to annoy people and your efforts will backfire."

### Think through policies and processes.

"Once you engage online, you're going to find fans and critics. Nonprofit groups know they can polarize audience opinions quickly. So be prepared. What will you do when someone starts criticizing you online? How will you handle attacks? Will you respond? If so — who responds, how, and in what form? How do you deal with well intentioned but off message fans? This is a complex area — seek out a consultant who has done this kind of work for other nonprofits or organizations and ask for their help. It will be worth it."

### Offer something of value.

"The incentive with HoHoTO was to have a great holiday party and be able to do some good at the same time. We created something of meaningful value for the community, and they rewarded us by showing up and giving very generously for the Daily Bread Food Bank. Simply tweeting about your great cause is not enough to really sustain people's interest — even the most charitable of us are still a little self-centered. With so many demands on our time and our pocketbooks, there has to be something valuable and worthwhile to make people want to really engage."

*Source: Michael O'Connor Clarke, Vice President, Thornley Fallis Communications, HoHoTO, Toronto, Ontario, Canada. Phone (416) 471-8664. E-mail: mocc@thornleyfallis.com*

**Promotion Idea**

Design attention-grabbing invitations that do more than simply announce your event.

ADMIT ONE

## 74. Appreciation-themed Events Build Goodwill, Publicity and Future Attendance

Once your event is over, look for ways to thank its key players that will further generate goodwill and publicity. Offering your special event's volunteers, sponsors or key supporters a thank-you gift — while expecting nothing in return — helps strengthen loyalty and goodwill that will inevitably be paid back through word-of-mouth publicity and future attendance. Here are ideas for doing so:

✓ **Give a custom gift basket**. Contact them by phone, postcard or e-mail to give them a choice of items such as gourmet coffee, chocolates, nuts or sugar free candy; sparkling cider or champagne; plus tickets to an upcoming event or free admission to your facilities for themselves and a friend.

✓ **Offer professional lessons**. Buy a group of your most dedicated supporters an hour-long session with their choice of a makeup artist, wardrobe consultant, golf pro, investment consultant or home staging professional. Look for experts who appeal to almost everyone in your database.

✓ **Create a spa escape**. Hire professionals with portable massage chairs or tables, manicure stations, facials or foot rubs. Include services that appeal to both genders and all ages. Offer light refreshments like calming teas, savory salads and whole grain breads. Choose a relaxing venue such as a large atrium with natural light, running water and plants. Send gift certificates to those who can't come.

✓ **Host a brunch and photo event**. Invite clients/donors and families for Sunday brunch at a hotel or banquet facility, followed by a photo session for the family, individuals or even a baby. Give them one photo as a gift — in a frame with your logo — and the option to purchase more poses from the photographer.

### Advertise Event's Universal Appeal

Don't leave potential guests wondering what your event has in store. Tell them in no uncertain terms. For example, to encourage the entire community to attend Art Under the Stars, the Fresno (CA) Art Museum circulates an open invitation in an easy conversational tone.

## 75. Host Grand Openings With Local Flair

A fun, festive, well-organized grand opening will leave a long-lasting positive impression with your guests. Take your grand opening a step further to emphasize the positive aspects of your city or region, celebrate your community and draw more attendees. To do so:

✓ Offer free local samplings. Play up the grandest aspects of your region with locally grown or produced food and drink. Post information sheets that detail the local connection.

✓ Invite a local expert to speak on a topic related to your organization. Check in with the chamber for recommendations on lively presenters in your area.

✓ Create a business-to-business grand opening offering special discounts or trial memberships to other business professionals in your community to promote your dedication to local membership.

✓ Work with organizations aligned with your goals to showcase all resources and organizations in your region. Consider hosting a co-grand opening with these other organizations.

✓ Set the mood by inviting local musicians to play at the grand opening — a lyricist who can set the mood with up-tempo music, regional talent playing throughout the day, a local songwriter who can create and premiere a theme song for your organization.

### ADMIT ONE

### Promotion Idea

Include a sampling of fabulous items that will be auctioned off in promotional materials.

## 76. Use Buses to Gain Attendance

You may have the entertainment, prizes and food lined up, but your event won't have much success if your guests can't make it. "Many guests may not come if they can't find parking or walking distance is too great," says Vic Laxson, general manager of the destination management company Hello Florida! (Orlando, FL). That's why bussing in guests may help an event run more smoothly and increase turnout.

Laxson suggests asking yourself these questions when deciding whether to use a bus service:

- Does the event location have sufficient parking for the number of expected guests?
- Does the event involve multiple facilities?
- How far is the walk from the parking area to the event site? Is it too far for guests to walk?
- Are your guests being transferred from a hotel to an off-site location?

If you still aren't sure whether bussing is right for your event, put yourself in an attendee's shoes and walk through the entire event. "Consider weather, walking distance and traffic as you walk through the entire guest experience. If there are challenges leading up to your guests arrival, it will greatly diminish their overall experience. You only get one chance to make both the first and last impressions, and transportation can be key to both," says Laxson.

When deciding where to have drop off/pick-up locations, Laxon says to keep in mind the distance attendees will have to walk in case of bad weather, the area where your guests will wait for buses, the number of buses that are able to fit in the pick-up/drop off location, and the traffic flow in the pick-up/drop off location and along the route.

Once you've found a good company, give them as much information as possible about the event, including event flow, event times, number of expected guests and time frame. "This information affords the transportation management company the ability to give you an accurate quote. Without it they will likely give you a worst case estimate which is based on all guests arriving and departing at the same time. This type of transfer requires the most vehicles and results in a higher per-person cost," Laxson says.

Documenting your attendance history is the best way to manage costs, says Laxson. "Knowing how many people you transfer and the approximate times will give you the information you need to schedule more efficiently in the future," he says. If you're bussing in people from a distance, you may want to consider factoring in the cost of transportation into the ticket cost for your event. The cost of event transportation can vary, but typically it costs between $10 and $20 per person for groups of 50 people.

*Source: Vic Laxson, General Manager, Hello Florida!, Orlando, FL. Phone (407) 674-3002. E-mail: vlaxson@hello-florida.com. Website: www.hello-usa.com*

### How Often Should Busses Run?

"The key to timing is communication. Many events run shuttles every 15, 20 or 30 minutes. The key is setting the expectation with the guests so they can plan their arrival and departure. We recommend that every group allows for some buses to run all evening long for emergencies, weather, attendees with small children, or any reason that people would want/or need to leave early. The number of buses that run all night does vary per event based on distance between the venue and the hotel, the turnaround time and the flow of the event."

— *Vic Laxson, GM, Hello Florida! (Orlando, FL)*

Lightning Source UK Ltd.
Milton Keynes UK
UKOW011858280613

212924UK00006B/153/P